Edited by Barbara Goličnik
Marušić, Matej Nikšič and Lise Coirier

HUMAN CITIES:
CELEBRATING
PUBLIC SPACE

stichting
kunstboek

HUMAN CITIES / celebrating public space

This publication has been released in the framework of the European project Human Cities: Celebrating public space (2008-2010), supported by the EU programme Culture 2007-2013. It has been launched at the Human Cities Festival, Brussels, in May 2010.

The Human Cities Network is composed of Institut supérieur d'Architecture de la Communauté française de Belgique La Cambre (BE) — *Jean-Louis Genard, Chantal Vanoeteren, Cécile Stas, Sabine Guisse, Rafaella Houlstan.* Pro Materia (BE) — *Lise Coirier, Zoé Vantournhoudt, Claude-Julie d'Huart.* The Lighthouse (UK) — *Ali Bell, Lori Mc Elroy.* Politecnico di Milano (IT) — *Ezio Manzini, Anna Meroni, Paola Trapani, François Jegou, Giampiero Pitisci.* Urban Planning Institute of the Republic of Slovenia (SLO) — *Barbara Goličnik Marušić, Matej Nikšič, Nina Goršič, Biba Tominc.* With the expertise of Culture Lab (BE) — *Gian Giuseppe Simeone, Alexis Castro.* In collaboration with Cité du design (FR).

www.humancities.eu

CONTENTS

PREFACE

Lise Coirier

Human Cities, as a project and as a phenomenon, offers innovative perspectives of and contributions to the public space, which is emerging as a realm of creative intervention and collaboration between artists, designers, architects, sociologists, writers, philosophers, urban planners and landscape architects. Research aims to provide reliable empirical data that can be used to create urban public space.

Since its launch in November 2008, the Human Cities network has contributed to the emergence of 'creative cities', laboratories for informal, temporary, creative performances and installations of static or dynamic forms and objects that challenge our existing art, architecture and design stereotypes. The network has raised awareness of the need for more systematic research into the less obvious components of public space such as social networks, behavioural patterns and perceptual dimensions. It has also emphasized sustainability and creativity in urban design as crucial to educational and participative programmes for the broad public of urban spaces.

With an objective to enter the city design process from as many perspectives as possible, this project hopes to expand the network in the future, through this publication and by sharing the project with more cities in Europe and at the intercontinental level.

INTRODUCTION

Matej Nikšič and Barbara Goličnik Marušić

Rapid technological development, socio-cultural challenges and environmental issues are severely transforming our lives. Change is the only constant. Nevertheless, people throughout history have had similar notions, no matter how those periods were assessed later. What this historically omnipresent notion might reflect is a common human belief in change as fundamental to human existence.

What distinguishes different historical periods and cultures from each other is a focal point where the endeavours for change are most intense. In Western society, the Industrial Revolution has been understood as the improvement of the material representation of the world to a great extent. It aimed to provide the fundamentals of a more pleasant life by producing new and better means to achieve well-being. Constant technological improvement allowed production to exceed peoples' needs over time. At the same time, consumption gained in importance. In 1976, Erich Fromm discussed the two different orientations - towards *to have* and towards *to be*. Today they seem to have culminated in *I consume, therefore I am* and *The more I consume, the more I am*. Consuming has become one of the basic components of the socio-economic foundation of Western society.

Nevertheless, consumption-based progress is being fundamentally questioned. It has many negative effects on the environment, social structures and economic relations, and it fails to provide a feeling of happiness to many of its 'beneficiaries'. A shift away from blind production and consumption is being deliberated and alternatives proposed.

In this context, progress is no longer seen in strictly material terms. The physical environment has been overexploited, and humanity's role in the ecological system is gaining attention. New theoretical frameworks and practical initiatives aim to (re)think the foundations of the world we live in. As the world population is becoming more and more urban, many of these theories and initiatives focus on urban living. Disciplines are approaching the creation of urban environments in a holistic and interdisciplinary way to ensure future development that will balance the environmental, social and economic aspects of urban living.

In these endeavours, the public space plays an increasingly important role. It is a sphere where many aspects of sustainable urban development can be fulfilled, not only in environmental and social terms, but also in moral terms. New patterns of urban living are imposing new demands on cities, of which public spaces represent a fundamental part. Urban public spaces are being rethought and re-conceptualized, attributed new content, formats and forms, and even being dematerialized and set up in a virtual world. Roles in the creation of urban public spaces are also being reconsidered.

These changes are reflected in the contributions to this book, whose aim is far from providing another definition of what is (or is not) the urban public space. The editors' intention is rather to show what is happening in spheres related to the urban public space: theoretical approaches to better understand and explain urban public space; practical approaches to conceptualizing and designing it; and actual initiatives that are unfolding in Europe and worldwide.

The book is the result of collaboration between five institutions and their partners within the project Human Cities: Sustainable Urban Design, which is funded by the EU Culture 2007-2013 Programme. It has opened the door to extensive collaborations between the Architecture and Design Centre (formerly, The Lighthouse), Glasgow, Scotland; La Cambre Architecture School, Brussels, Belgium; Department INDACO (Industrial Design) of Politecnico di Milano, Milan, Italy; Pro Materia Creative Design Consultancy Agency, Brussels; and the Urban Planning Institute of the Republic of Slovenia, Ljubljana.

Organized into four main parts, the book is an overview of contemporary public space issues raised through the Human Cities project. Part One, *Public for place*, reflects on how design theory and practice can conceive and develop feasible solutions to create unprecedented forms of community and public spaces in cities. It examines the complexity of contemporary society and cities that are considered laboratories, where new ideas and solutions are being invented. Examples prove the emergence of a new field of design that – as Ezio Manzini points out – supports social innovation in the construction of public space.

Part Two, *Place for public*, pays greater attention to actual users in a concrete physical open space of the city. It searches for ways to combine the design of a physical layout of any concrete space with the so-called soft attributes of space, such as user needs and habits, and their perceptions and expectations of a space. Part Two also addresses geographic information systems (GIS) as a practical tool to establish an urban public space database that can serve anyone interested in or in need of detailed and cross-referenced empirical knowledge related to public space.
Part Three, *Public in place*, provides insight by delving into

what is happening in the real world. It reveals the broad range of contemporary knowledge of urban public space, which can be understood as a concrete physical space, a platform for interaction or even as an ongoing negotiation process among interested parties. It also stresses the importance of focusing on specific groups of users and illustrates it through children and youth case studies.

Part Four, *Public space as a common good*, presents 30 projects selected from 70 submissions to the world-wide Call for Entries launched by the Human Cities project in spring 2009. Part Four represents the most artistic part of the book by showing contemporary projects from around the globe. Videos and photographs, installations and urban performances communicated these new ideas, they are presented with texts and graphics in this book.

The editors would like to thank the authors and all those who contributed to this book, which is a collective endeavour that we believe contributes to the celebration of public space!

I. / PUBLIC FOR PLACE

Ezio Manzini

THE SOCIAL CONSTRUCTION OF PUBLIC SPACE

Ultimately, the history of cities is the history of two structurally correlated systems, one social and one material: the material city and the social city generate each other. At times, one of the two poles may look more dynamic and carry the other forward, but the evolution of one cannot be separated from that of the other.

Up to now, academics and designers have always focused on the material city, seeing it as a collection of buildings, products and infrastructure. They did, and are still doing, so because they have been convinced that the social city would adapt to fit, regenerating itself alone and without design, in a quasi-natural fashion. And, as a matter of fact, things have effectively always functioned in this way. However, something happened in the last century that forces us to look at cities in a different way: the speed and enormity of the changes which occurred, and are still taking place, broke with an age-old mechanism of quasi-natural mutual adaptation. This has led to an unprecedented crisis in cities themselves and, almost as an indicator of this more general crisis, the catastrophic deterioration of public spaces.

Confronted with such a situation, academics and designers are shifting their attention, and issues relating to the social city, i.e. to the communities and interconnected networks that make up a city, are attracting increasing interest. This has led us to observe the social phenomena taking place in cities, and in society at large, more attentively. Examining the complexity and contradictory nature of contemporary society, we find that cities are like huge social laboratories where new ideas and new solutions are being invented and experimented within all fields of daily life: food networks based on de-intermediated relationships between city and country; models of housing with shared facilities and services, and different forms of co-housing; mobility systems using appropriate alternative means of transport instead of individual cars; health and disease-prevention services based on active, collaborative roles for those concerned; cultural and recreational activities that lead to the generation of new forms of community and a new sense of citizenship (many examples of which can be found at http://www. desis-network.org and http://www.sustainable-everyday. net). These are feasible solutions that have already been implemented and, as a side-effect, are generating unprecedented forms of community (elective communities) and public spaces (shared public spaces). Ultimately, they suggest the potential emergence of a convivial, welcoming, safe city created by its own inhabitants. We can ask ourselves whether and how this potentiality can be made reality. In other words, whether and how the promising signs it is based on can be reinforced through specific design intervention. The answer to this question, as we shall see, may be encouraging. However, it is not an easy answer. In fact, communities and social networks, like all human systems (fortunately), cannot be designed as if they were buildings or material infrastructure. What we can think of and indeed create are suitable *enabling solutions.* In other words, we can design the material (and even the economic and regulatory) conditions that could make the development of such a city more probable.

The seven chapters that make up the first part of the book are a series of reflections on and examples of how design theory and practice can conceive and develop such enabling solutions. In *Social innovation, collaborative networks and public space*, Anna Meroni and Paola Trapani discuss how design may be able to support *creative communities* in their capacity to invent and put into practice new ways of living and new forms of public space. In *Active urban scenes*, Boštjan Bugarič suggests the potentialities of *creative practices*: participatory social events that counteract the current tendency to conform to standard practice. In *A welcoming city*, Luisa Collina introduces the concept of diffused hospitality as a strategy for creating a greater and more mutually constructive understanding between local residents and tourists. In *Residencies in public institutions supporting local transition to sustainable ways of living*, François Jégou and Stéphane Vincent present a programme in which multidisciplinary teams are included in local administrations with the aim of activating a process of participatory design. In *Pedagogical tool kit to investigate social innovation in urban environments: the LOLA project*, Giampiero Pitisci presents a tool to help schools adopt effective practices and present themselves as agents of change and advocates of a new kind of public space. In *Volunteered geography as a driver for community-based services*, Serena Pollastri proposes a participatory geography project that seeks to involve communities in the production of local area maps and, at the same time, to make the maps into an opportunity for creating new communities. Finally, in *Cartography as a common good*, Rafaella Houlstan-Hasaerts and Nicolas Malevé approach maps as a tool for spurring communities to reconsider their local area and influence its future.

All of these reflections and proposals indicate not only the emergence of a new field for design – supporting social innovation in the construction of public space – they also outline a new way of designing. The seven contributions that we present here clearly demonstrate this. Each combines a territorial, strategic design project, which we can call the *framework project,* with numerous small and medium scale interventions, the *local projects,* which are interconnected but at the same time able to function autonomously. What emerges is a *design plan* in which a wider programme is supported and made concrete by a series of local, flexible, quickly implementable initiatives.

All of this is particularly important for the issue of public space and its designability. Anna Meroni and Paola Trapani write in their article that public space is 'the accessible field of opportunity and interaction, where people can meet to share experiences and visions, where they can try out new paths to solve their own problems and improve the quality of life.' Therefore, if public space is the place where different activities can take place, its construction must follow a similar model: a complex construction that emerges from a design plan whose meaning and enabling potentials emerge from a network of independent but interconnected activities.

AUTHORS / Anna Meroni and Paola Trapani

CHAPTER / Social innovation, collaborative networks
and public space*

* this essay is the result of a collective work, but for the purpose of this publication, the sub-chapters one, three, five have been written by A. Meroni, and the sub-chapters two and four have been written by P. Trapani.

INTRODUCTION

This essay presents a *social innovation*-led approach to designing public space. Assuming social innovation as a significant change in the way individuals or communities act, often as a bottom-up initiative, in order to produce a result, it discusses the motivations that spur groups or communities to take action regarding public space, and how design can support them.

This perspective implies the power of the social fabric to shape the meaning and structure of a physical public space, instead of the other way round.

The action of (re)shaping is a real opportunity to enhance the conception of *public space as a common good* in contemporary cities, one that must remain at the full disposal of all members of a community as inseparable social and spatial elements. The frail substance of this kind of common good is continuously subject to attack when the sense of community and empowerment is lost.

We propose reflecting on the role of *creative communities* and *collaborative networks* in creating and promoting new typologies of public space, by discussing a number of cases where spaces and common services are shared and opened to their neighbourhoods; local resources and skills are connected to a wider network; and initiatives aim to promote the value of a territory.

THE POWER AND POTENTIAL OF CREATIVE COMMUNITIES

Research into Creative Communities has, so far, a consolidated background that we have matured over the years[1] collecting and analysing cases of social innovation from all over the world. We call *Creative Communities* groups of people who creatively organize themselves in ways that promise concrete steps towards sustainable living and producing. They represent a kind of social innovation that can drive technological and production innovation in view of sustainability (Meroni 2007).

Focussing on communities has led us to talk about *Community Centred Design,* where the attention shifts from the individual user to the community as the new subject of interest for a design that is more conscious of current social dynamics (Meroni 2008).

Many lessons have been learnt from this experience. One of the most interesting, meaningful and, to some extent, surprising is the deep, lasting and identity-building sense of enjoyment and satisfaction in taking care of people/things/places and in putting effort into doing things. Both are ways of taking responsibility for the community and society in general and thus the common good, including public space. This is where the importance of creating a *social innovation*-led approach for design has become crucial: as designers, we can do a lot to launch, support and spread its application. Within a society where pleasure and well-being are mainly conceived (and proposed) as being served and consuming goods, this lesson is an equivalent of a Copernican Revolution: it can trigger a new way of conceiving and developing innovation across social and business fields.

The process behind this behaviour, according to psychologists (Seligman & Csikszentmihalyi 2000), lies at the root of self-fulfilment. Subjective well-being is related to a belief in interpersonal relationships: the capacity to unite people around an idea, to motivate them, to convene to resolve a problem are therefore ways of building community values and instilling a sense of personal well-being. An attitude of this kind occurs when we stop seeing ourselves as consumers and discover that we are able to determine our own lives; when we make creative use of objects in the plenitude of society, according to what Inghilleri (2003) calls 'sense endowed materialism', using artefacts instead of being used by them.

As a natural consequence, sensibility towards the common good increases and all *commons* acquire a new importance in the personal and collective sense of well-being and belonging.

This tendency is also evident in what we can call the *emerging economy*,[2] which is founded on three pillars:
– a social character that is closely linked to the social innovation we have been studying;
– environmental re-orientation that leads to a green revolution and a new territorial focus;
– technological innovation that comes from an unprecedented technological breakthrough.

Such an economy calls for a new notion of goods to support solutions enabling people to build the lives they want to live. It is neither products nor services that are valued most, but the support that helps people lead their lives as they wish and navigate a complex world. Manzini (2010) talks about 'platforms for actions' enabling people to express themselves and bring their own capabilities into play to create the solutions in their own lives, becoming part

of the answer rather than part of the problem. Here, services acquire a unique importance: service provision rather than goods is becoming fundamental to economic exchange.[3] Value is co-created with and defined by the user, rather than embedded in outputs, and that is why services become the paradigm of this emerging economy (Meroni & Sangiorgi 2010).

PUBLIC SPACE AS A SPECIAL KIND OF COMMON GOOD

The Social Economy is also characterized by: a strong role for values and missions in groups active in certain fields; an emphasis on collaboration and repeated interactions to accomplish bottom-up actions aiming to achieve a common goal; a preference for care and maintenance rather than one-off consumption; blurring boundaries between production and consumption; the intensive use of distributed networks to sustain and manage relationships capable of being conducted via broadband, mobile and other means of communication (Murray 2009).

Public space seems to be one of the favourite hot spots of this economy and of social innovation, given its intrinsic nature as space of and for relationships.

We went straight to the point by defining public space as a special type of common good. Public space is traditionally common, a resource collectively owned. We believe that the novelty lies in considering it from a broader perspective that includes not only the spatial

sphere but the cultural and behavioural ones as well, in a holistic vision of what a 'common good' is. Thus it is the public space in tandem with what happens (or could happen) in it that reflects its true significance to the community. Public space is therefore both a social, political and physical space 'where things get done and where people have a sense of belonging and have an element of control over their lives'.[4]

It undeniably promotes the values and the missions shared by the local community, fostering a sense of identity and belonging. Public places are the accessible fields of opportunity and interaction, where people can meet to share experiences and visions, explore new paths to solve their problems and improve their quality of life. Given its inherent character of accessibility, public space is the natural stage for social interaction and collaboration, generating buzz, exerting reciprocal influence and imparting unexpected delight in the most dynamic neighbourhoods of our cities. Conversely, the meaning of public space is continuously eroded when the sense of being a group of empowered people with a common interest and living together in a given place is lost. Suddenly, public space loses its 'good' status, becoming a no man's land, a place of fear, crime, pollution and degradation.

In recent decades, the ability to reshape urban space according to new needs has been an effective way to promote an attitude of caring and maintenance rather than opportunistic consumption. The topic of land waste is certainly crucial in the present environmental crisis, but the rising awareness of its limited availability can prevent disappointed citizens from moving to the countryside only if the community is able to make cities desirable places to live in.

While other kinds of common goods, such as air and water, are given resources, public space is commonly produced. For this reason its meaning, allocation and use has to respect the needs of a vast audience. The creativity of those who live in and manage cities will determine the latter's future success and attractiveness. However, we often forget that creativity is not an exclusive domain of artists and innovation isn't exclusively technological. The emerging paradigm shifts attention toward social innovation, which takes place, most of the time, in the commonly produced good of public space (Landry 2000).

WHAT MOTIVATES INFORMAL GROUPS TO TAKE ACTION REGARDING PUBLIC SPACE

When considering public space as a unit where meaning, spatial context, and social and technical conditions produced by groups of active citizens are inseparable, the conventional boundary criteria of private and public goods become obsolete: since the first lies within the realm of the market and the other pertains to the state, they no longer seem useful when it comes to considering social innovation.

It has been argued[5] that today social innovation stems from many sources: for instance, new forms of mutual action between individuals within the household economy – whether in the form of open source software, or web-based social networking around specific issues – are increasing and gaining relevance. Generally speaking, the household is becoming a fundamental cell of social innovation.

Moreover, the development of social enterprise operating within the market has been noticeable (Jégou & Manzini 2008; Murray 2009). Reaching beyond the limitations of the old categories, we discover that the market can, to some extent, meet the goals of the social economy.[6]

It is also true that the state is reshaping the concept of public property and the way to 'commensurate' social production, changing its own methods of allocation and control. In other cases, in addition to producing sociality, innovation by social enterprises has provoked responses from the private sector and the state. Finally, the weight of the household within the social economy, as mentioned above, is growing through either labour in the household and the contribution to social production of informal networks, associations and social movements, and these comprise the realm of the social production of public space.

The following is a list of the most common motivations for the actions of informal groups in public spaces. It is not exhaustive; nevertheless, it is useful to sort the enormous variety of case studies into groups according to common characteristics.

Of course, case studies can match one or more of these categories:

– *to produce goods for the household economy* – the household sub-economy and the extension of family productive space into public space, as in an extended home, i.e. allotment gardens and community gardens;

– *to host services and activities shared by community housing* – the public space of a neighbourhood community formally or informally structured as co-housing, i.e. playgrounds for children, barter and yard markets, open access workplaces;

– *to create contexts in which elective communities can express themselves, get organized and find synergies to help each other* – the realm of public art and of amateur activities, e.g. flash mobs, artistic performances, sport sessions, knitting activities, music performances;

– *to reclaim the streets for different uses* – the city re-appropriated for more human activities, e.g. proximity-vacation spots, spaces to rest and relax, public dining tables, public dancing floors, cycling and walking areas, open-air cinemas;

– *to express a political position, through activities and/or art performances* – public space as a context of constructive protest, cultural and social engagement, where proposals are presented through demonstrative prototypes of possible improvements, e.g. guerrilla gardening, reforestation initiatives;

– *to enhance living contexts* – public space as an everyday panorama that calls for quality beyond the distinction between public and private, e.g. loan gardens cultivated by neighbours; cleaning days and public space maintenance by

residents; open museums and galleries;
– *to improve security and safety* – public space as 'neighbourhood concierge', with infrastructure maintained by residents, i.e. neighbourhood watch and maintenance services.

NETWORKING AND CONNECTING

While conducting our research, we observed the presence of groups of citizens working in different urban contexts to raise the local community's awareness of public space.[7] We see these creative groups as collectively playing the role of hero, even though they simply perceive in advance what will later become a common opinion.

Given the blurred boundary between public space production and consumption, we can borrow Alvin Toffler's term 'prosumer'[8] to define the new kind of aware citizen who knows what the right solutions are for his/her local situation. Without prosumer action, the mere physical public space is as useful as a piece of hardware without software. The community is the context in which to orchestrate this plurality of voices through a democratic process that recognizes equal opportunities to all members and allows their desires to guide the creation and implementation of solutions.

The present stage of transformative innovation would not be possible without the spread of global infrastructure for communication and social networking. We have already mentioned the circular relationship between physical space and the people living in it, but public spaces are now being redefined and extended thanks to a third applied force: information and communication technology (ICT). Flash mobs, street festivals, publicly displayed televisions, and social groups of all kinds are the new high-tech actors of the wired public space. Terms like *peer-to-peer*, *disintermediation*, *wikis*, *collaborative platforms*, and *open source* have moved from the lexicon of distributed systems to the parlance of everyday life. It is interesting to observe the shift toward new habits, when people are given the tools to do things together without needing traditional top-down organizational structures.

Producing/consuming a new concept of public space has generated real everyday behaviours that are deeply influenced by the adoption and use of new communication technologies.

According to Shirky's rationale (Shirky 2009), social networking has changed users' attitude towards:
– CONNECTING with friends, family, and/or stakeholders who share interests, values and beliefs;
– COLLABORATING with others to accomplish a shared goal, vision or project;
– CONSUMING content to learn, be entertained, seek validation, or feel more connected;
– SHARING things (and values) they find interesting or important with friends, family and followers;
– CREATING content (photographs, videos, blog posts, tweets, comments) of various kinds to express themselves.

To varying degrees the case studies we have collected from around the world show these attitudes to be ingredients in the production of public space. They can be top-down initiatives, as in the case of the Big Heartworm (Minhoção) in São Paulo, where the Municipality closes the Elevado Costa e Silva, a violent wound in the city, on Sundays and opens it to the public for ciclovia-style recreation. However, they more often emerge as bottom-up actions, compliant with the current legislative body to a varying extent, as is the case in Milan, Italy, where 'guerrilla gardening' is an unofficial effort to embellish neglected or forgotten areas with plants and flowers. Between the two extremes we find cases where the municipality and the local community are engaged in a joint project, such as the 'Neighbourhood Shares' project at The Hague in the Netherlands, where residents have taken over responsibility from local authorities for certain neighbourhood maintenance tasks.

TOOLS FOR DOING AND SUPPORT

We need to question the role of the designer in this context. Definitely, it is time to adopt new perspectives.

It is time to *do things with people* and to *support people in doing things*. Both situations imply a co-designing capacity that must be put into practice with professional skills and tools.

Each and every kind of activity (connecting, collaborating, consuming, sharing, creating) raises potential design questions that fall into these two possible design roles; nevertheless, there are more transversal reflections that can be developed.

The capacity to build constructive relations with people and artefacts, so well revealed in the case of public space, can be enhanced by services designed to help people feel active and integrated within the context. Stimulating a positive attitude, systematically building competency and encouraging proactivity also helps prevent the whole of society from losing the meanings of its choices and behaviours.

It is important to show that firm commitment and hard work does bring a reasonable chance of success. We can start by considering the *collaborative* way in which behaviours such as taking care and making an effort take place. At present, collaboration and networking are the only feasible and effective ways for these initiatives to work: mutual support, resource sharing and group empowerment are the key elements of both their existence and their success. Basically, designers conceive tools to facilitate interaction with the environment: artefacts that possess utility and function, embody culture and induce emotion. What kind of tools, whether material or conceptual, can be designed to facilitate mutual support, allow resource sharing and create empathy within the community? The answer depends on the specific field of intervention, but, considering both the atavistic and relational nature of public space and the variety of cases observed so far, we can assume the hypothesis (Leadbeater 2008) that the nature of these tools has to be a peculiar mixture of the 'peasant and the geek', the pre-industrial and the post-industrial. Therefore, marrying advanced technology support to a hands-in-the-soil mindset – thereby linking the past with the future – has the potential to make people feel and be active and engaged in the contemporary world.

---

[1] Emerging User Demands for Sustainable Solutions (EMUDE); EU VI Framework Programme, 2004-06; Creative Communities for Sustainable Lifestyles (CCSL), a project promoted by the Task Force on Sustainable Lifestyles, within the United Nations Ten-Year Framework of Programmes on Sustainable Consumption and Production, 2005-07; Looking for Likely Alternatives (LOLA) Project within the framework of the EU Consumer Citizens Network (CCN), 2005-09; several academic courses, workshops and national research.

[2] According to different authors this is also defined as 'Social Economy' (Murray 2009; Murray Mulgan, Caulier-Grice 2008), 'Support Economy' (Shoshana & Maxmin 2002), 'Co-production Economy' (Leadbeather 2008; Von Hippel 2005; Ramirez 1999; Vargo & Lush 2004), 'Next Economy' (Manzini in Meroni & Sangiorgi 2010).

[3] See Vargo & Lush 2004, Vargo, Maglio & Archpru Akaka 2008.

[4] N Hildyard, C Hines & T Lang, 'Who Competes? Changing Landscapes of Corporate Control', The Ecologist, vol. 26, no. 4, July/August 1996.

[5] C Leadbeater, We Think, Profile Books, Ltd., London, 2008; R Murray, G Mulgan, J Caulier-Grice, 'How to Innovate: The tools for social innovation', working paper. SIX, Social Innovation Exchange, UK, 2008.

[6] This is the purpose of much recent environmental policy that seeks to redefine the responsibilities of private property: the Toyota Roof Garden Corporation is an example of a post-Fordist private company focused on restoring the loss of vegetation in urban areas, which has been causing not only the heat-island effect, air pollution, drought, and flooding, but also the loss of liveable public space.

[7] Groups like Rebar in San Francisco, esterni in Milan, Prostorož in Ljubljana, Future Canvas in Melbourne.

[8] A Toffler, The Third Wave, Collins, London, 1980.

AUTHOR / Boštjan Bugarič

CHAPTER / **Active urban scenes**

THE CONSTRAINTS OF URBAN PLANNING IN THE CONTEMPORARY CITY

Urbanization in contemporary cities is characterized by wild development resulting in the uniformity of public space. Diversity is subordinate to the interest of capital. Single-sense areas without any room for the development of diverse programmes are being organized without the slightest consideration of city user social networks. According to Jacobs (1972), four criteria have to be met to stimulate urban diversity: multi-functionality, small size of housing blocks, intertwinement of buildings from various ages and concentration of users. Diversity is a crucial prerequisite for the development of a city's urbanity. Contrary to the established hierarchical and rigid planning procedures, it is sensible to introduce flexible developmental principles, conceived on the basis of the requirements of city users. The grounds for this type of planning are defined by Lefebvre (1986) as the 'right to the city' which prevents programme dispersal. Lefebvre (1986) argues that the basis for the creation of a specific city

character lies in appropriate infrastructural interconnection of the existing built structures and new requirements of urban life. The concept presented in his competition project for the renovation of Novi Beograd associates and intertwines the existing built environment and emphasizes the diversity of programme.

In the neoliberal contemporary city public space is organized at the level of economic and political interests. Urban planning is adapted to the interests of investors and capital. Mumford (1961) states that we are living in an age of self-destruction of urban environment with cities exploding into amorphous masses of urban remains as a result of consumerist imperatives taking effect. Thus urban planning has become a way of appropriating the natural and the built environment. The opposite of the capitalist way of organizing the city is the possibility of active participation through creative (artistic) practices. These (re)create urban scenes accommodating programme, which stimulates the building up of sensitivity of the wider public awareness of urban issues. Hočevar (2000) defines urban scenes as places that house (un)intentionally constructed events in public spaces and in private spaces with

public access. The mutual communication of various actors results in deliberately targeted events promoting the formation of active urban scenes and making them more attractive to users. The re-urbanization processes employed by contemporary city investors include four developmental strategies of renovation: gentrification is taking action to attract the middle and higher social classes back into the old city centres and city quarters with problematic demographic structures; cityzation or business-driven revitalization signifies the transformation of a city centre into a business district; conservation represents the physical renovation of the built structure within the sphere of monument preservation; touristification is spatially-functional transformation of the city to serve the purposes of tourism.

Gentrification is implemented with the objective of refining the uniform demographic structure of city users. Capital investments into lower class residential areas induces their transformation into upper class residential areas. The result is total transformation of the social structure, a sort of capital-driven cleaning of neglected areas. Touristification has a negative effect on urban diversity. The excess development of activities related to tourism results in monotony. Common to both developmental strategies is the ambition to attract large capital investments in the shortest time possible without considering the needs of city users.

THE SPACE OF PUBLIC PARTICIPATION

Public space is the foundation for the formation of public opinion. The privatization of urban public space is causing its transformation into a controlled environment of consumption. Urban planning cannot master and direct the development according to public needs or expert guidelines, as it is tangled up in investor interests. Reforms linking expertise and economy are seizing its autonomy and its capacity to criticize poorly founded capital-driven spatial interventions. This sort of urban planning results in a particular form of representing public space which includes intentional managing of the society of its users. Activities taking place in these areas are carefully planned and sharply determined.

Informal action of civil society represents a form of resistance against the transformation of public space. Participative techniques of cultural practices address questions concerning various urban topics as means of inducing development of programmes in various urban environments. This prevents the development of a single type of activities by encouraging visits to certain urban areas, which are facing abandonment due to various urban,

social, and economic processes. Temporary installations, performances and urban actions organized in public space represented an answer to social, cultural, and spatial discordances. Independent events started to occur in urban scenes, which presented particular urban problems to the public while simultaneously encouraging the formation of public opinion. This actions are a beginning of The Situationist International movement, which began in the 1950's and 1960's. Within their scope, interactions, associations, interferences and interpretations of events are created and offered to the consideration of the wider public with the intention of creating new components of public space and thus forming a dynamic site of encounters. The situationists raised space-related questions through staging situationist events.

CREATIVE PRACTICES – EXAMPLES OF STAGING URBAN SCENES

The strategy of creative practices is reinforced with communication to increase the sensitisation of the public awareness. Temporary and swift interventions are often illegal, as they point to the erroneous regulation of public conduct. The concept of active urban scenes increase the attraction of the place and induce the consideration of issues associated with the site. In that way they become places with deliberately constructed events or spatial installations whose staging of events transforms their significance. Staging changes non-places to places and brings in all

symbolic expression displaying its character, relations or historical predispositions. Bauman (2002) claims that non-places are taking up an increasing proportion of physical space in spite of the fact that they are only meant for passing by and are usually quickly abandoned. Urban action plays the role of an indicator showing the state of a certain locality and making it possible to create social and spatial definitions as the process continues.

Creating urban scenes is a process of staging events in degraded ambiences as means of their presentation to the wider public with the purpose of their education and legitimising physical interventions (Bugarič, 2004). They establish a basis for implementing an integral strategy of stimulating urbanity. The problems associated with a chosen site are presented to the wider public on location with the purpose of educating and justifying physical interventions. Below, four examples of implementing this strategy are presented in a chronological sequence of performed events. All actions were organized and performed by C3 which had a role of an independent actor.

Example 1: Experimental revitalization

Location

An abandoned zinc factory complex is situated at the edge of the city centre of Celje. The industrial programme was terminated and the factory's architectural heritage had not been suitably evaluated, so this area was left to stagnate.

Creating urban scenes

New urban scenes of development include old industrial buildings housing temporary programmes. New activities provide public access to restricted urban areas, thus making possible their transformation into developmental centres. An attempt was made to attract the media to the location by staging a performance in the crumbling halls and

RELEVANCE	Ravitalisation of a degraded area
EFFECTIVENESS	Revitalization and increasing public recognition of the problem
EFFICIENCY	Informal presentation, action operation, attractive approach
IMPACT	A single event does not produce wanted effects
SUSTAINABILITY	Acquiring new areas for the spatial development of the city

Table 1: Assessing effects of the experiment according to the five principles in Celje.

underneath the tall brick chimneys of the old zinc factory. A spectator placed in the middle of this conflicted area discovered the location during the course of a performance by C3 in September 2000. By testing the efficiency of this experiment according to the five principles, it can be discerned that repeated action is an important factor, which contributes significantly to the effectiveness of the entire strategy.

Future

The epilogue of the old zinc factory's story was an urban design competition. The construction of a new Technopolis requires a

Figure 1: CC project, old zinc factory Celje.

large empty area, so the protected industrial architectural heritage was demolished.

Example 2: Opening up an empty cultural monument

Location

The second case study discusses the Servi di Maria Monastery in the city centre of Koper. The building complex has been crumbling physically due to the lack of suitable programme during the last ten years. This is a case of approaching

Figure 2: GOVORILNICA project in Koper.

RELEVANCE	New spatial concept of the city
EFFECTIVENESS	Raising awareness of the local community through public debate and support of the media
EFFICIENCY	Linking action operation and attractive presentation
IMPACT	Including the local public increases the credibility of the strategy
SUSTAINABILITY	Protecting the architectural heritage from ruin

Table 2: Assessing effects of the experiment according to the five principles in Koper.

an area with a suitable revitalization programme suggested by the local community, and then trying to identify the needs of local actors and meet them during realization.

Creating urban scenes

An urban action, following the strategy described above, was performed in the monastery atrium. The work process was oriented towards attracting as much

attention as possible to the selected urban area. Various local experts, co-creators of the city programme of Koper, were invited to present their views on this problem.

Future

The lack of information about intended urban interventions is a consequence of the uncontrolled planning process and of capital interests. In the atmosphere of general negligence this results in an organization of space that bypasses the interests of its residents. Through its educational function the strategy raises the level of awareness on the part of experts while simultaneously contributing to the creation of better coordination between informal actions of civil society. Four concept designing projects for setting up programmes have been elaborated for this monastery, but it is still abandoned.

Figure 3: WAITING ROOM projects in Ljubljana.

Example 3: Critical approach to the privatization of public space

Location

Both cases below are oriented towards observing the sphere of public space in different time intervals and taking a critical approach to the processes observed. The criticism is aimed at the gradual privatization of public space owing to the acceptance of neoliberal city governance. These tendencies can be observed in two squares in the centre of Ljubljana: Trg republike and Prešernov trg. The construction of provisional arrangements with defined programmes created new relationships within the public sphere and attracted visitors.

Creating urban scenes

Today, Trg republike is used as a parking lot and a transversal route for pedestrians. It is a non-place, where there is nothing to attract visitors. The construction of a provisional structure created a new urban scene in the square. The

RELEVANCE	Inappropriate use of programme/ intensive flow of city users
EFFECTIVENESS	Public presentation with assistance of the media/ good response of city users
EFFICIENCY	Attractive and complex presentation
IMPACT	Temporary structure
SUSTAINABILITY	Opening public space to the public

Table 3: Assessing effects of the experiment according to the five principles in Ljubljana.

Figure 4: 'Private property, do not enter': appropriating public space in Trieste.

Waiting Room, an interactive action in an urban environment, was composed of two parts: each day various activities would take place inside the provisional structure and simultaneously broadcast over the radio. Prešernov trg has a function, opposite to that of Trg republike, as its location is very easily accessed. The objective of setting up a provisional structure in Prešernov trg was to survey public opinion: visitors were invited to write down their comments on urban development.

Future

The problem of privatization of urban public space has developed on the basis of various factors. Individual actors involved tackle this problem both successfully and unsuccessfully. The above examples indicate that the planning of open public space in Ljubljana is still questionable. I would like to stress an example of inappropriate urban public space accessibility. The Piazza San Antonio Nuovo in Trieste is an example of the inappropriate management of public space. The entire area of a public square is appropriated by the church as an institution: the square is enclosed behind a fence with a sign.

Example 4: Comparative developmental analysis

Location

The last example illustrates a possibility of association among cultural institutions and independent groups in raising public awareness within different cities. The process enables the assembly of a network of actions and events that are independent of any institutions and provides some objective insight into urban issues. The examples of good practice include Urbanfestival in Zagreb, PAPs in Belgrade and Urbanity in Ljubljana.

Creating urban scenes

Associating authors and non-government organizations into informal networks outside institutions supports the attempts of solving problems by state institutions. An apparatus is constructed, which opens up communication among actors involved and thus creates an objective sphere of activity at the expert

RELEVANCE	Linking institutions - government and non-government sector
EFFECTIVENESS	Discussing the role and significance of contemporary architecture
EFFICIENCY	New way of communicating between experts and non-experts
IMPACT	Increasing attraction of cultural institutions
SUSTAINABILITY	Starting public debate

Table 4: Assessing effects of the experiment according to the five principles in the case of festivals.

Figure 5: Some urban scenes form festivals (Ljubljana, Zagreb, Belgrade).

level as well as the level of civil society. The main objective of the Urbanity project was to present the functioning of selected Central European cities at this moment in time and to suggest the establishment of new ways of communicating with the public. A string of exhibitions in all project cities has enabled the establishment of communication between independent architectural centres and galleries.

Future

This example indicates that informal action based on expertise and public opinion is potentially very efficient. This sort of action can form democratic public domains and assemble critical mass capable of articulating demands concerning urban issues.

CONCLUSION

The crucial starting point of any urban planning is the analysis of city user requirements with respect to city programme. Jacobs (1972) published her work nearly five decades ago; however, at that time the American cities considered in her analysis were strongly influenced by neoliberalism, which is now the case with many European cities. To establish a new developmental foundation, it is therefore reasonable to adopt an approach primarily concerned with city programme and only then undertakes the physical spatial design. It is important for city users to be acquainted with urban interventions and to be able to take part in the designing process. City programme is not supposed to develop in predetermined zones, as this prevents the spontaneous generation of diversity and results in uniformity of space, which does not inspire heterogeneity and thus urbanity. By creating active urban scenes we can emphasize certain urban problems before any interventions are made. This provides the basis for avoiding a common misconception among building specialists, according to which the situation within a pre-designed built environment will change as soon as it is populated by a community with a particular set of requirements and interactions, resulting in the instantaneous development of diversity.

AUTHOR / Luisa Collina

CHAPTER / **A welcoming city**

INTRODUCTION

A 'welcoming city' is able to attract international tourists and facilitate their integration into the local context, promoting the sharing of experiences and spaces between inhabitants and visitors. This idea of collaboration between hosts and guests within the welcoming city's public spaces is here defined as hospitality. Hospitality is a crucial element of accommodation. New models of hosting visitors include small scale units diffused within the physical as well as social territory. Designing accommodation that promotes and increases hospitality preserves the vitality of contemporary cities and supports the enhancement of their public spaces.

GUESTS AND HOSTS

During the Milan Furniture Fair and its related events, Milan promotes values and becomes beautiful in a way that is unapparent during the rest of the year. These activities have been recently branded 'Milan Design Week'. Motivated by an interest in design, visitors of all ages and backgrounds (students, famous professional designers and entrepreneurs) convene from all over the world to attend thousands of events (in public open spaces and often disused private places made accessible and beautiful only for this period) open to everyone. Local residents, artists and ordinary citizens curious about design participate, meet international visitors, attend presentations, exhibitions and performances, and discover places that are normally closed.

The world's most attractive and dynamic cities are able to flourish not only during specific events but repeatedly throughout the year. Welcoming cities attract visitors of all ages, interests and economic resources from all over the world and offer them the possibility of experiencing the local culture, discovering hidden places and establishing new relations, not only with other tourists, but mainly with the residents. Tourism on these terms is important to the city, and is based on three main pillars: hosts, guests and places where:

– the host lives happily in a place where he/she is proud to invite a guest;
– the guest who accepts the host's invitation is eager to establish a relationship with him/her;
– the place is a physical, social and cultural context generated by the host and enriched by the guest.[1]

Public spaces in this context recover the role of a physical and symbolic meeting place for guests and hosts: attractive places that express local historical and cultural values, but that also invite relaxation and are well-suited to entertain and host events.

Supporting tourism, especially incoming flows, and guiding foreign guests not only to the main attractions in the city centre, but also to discover interesting localities elsewhere in the territory is a strategic way of increasing the vitality of contemporary cities and assuring public spaces their important role as a crossroads for individuals and cultures.

This kind of tourism (defined in the following text as *hospitality*) makes an important contribution to the regeneration of local territorial capital, valorizing host places, offering residents new economical and entrepreneurial opportunities, and promoting new, significant opportunities for intercultural relationships between guests and hosts.

Leaders who want their cities to remain attractive in the global competition to play a welcoming role internationally have to respond to new tourism behaviours and demands. Their goal should be to diversify by catering to the countless varieties of individual demands rather than to focus on one specific (high) target; to develop new solutions that are economically accessible to young people and families with low and middle incomes, and not only to businessmen with deep pockets; to find ways of integrating local communities and foreigners rather than keeping them in two separate environments without any possibility of sharing experiences; to lead tourists throughout the territory rather than limiting them to city centres.

Accommodation is a very important issue for travellers: financially, it's one of the most significant costs of a trip, and psychologically, it's what makes a tourist feel at home and welcome, or isolated and rejected. But while where to spent the night is a key question that influences traveller destinations, the accommodation industry, deaf to the new demands, continues to present very traditional models of hospitality.

To move forward in terms of accommodation, welcoming cities must offer solutions that are:
– highly diverse and thus able to meet the increasingly heterogeneous demand;
– 'flexible' to changing flows of arrivals over the course of the year;
– 'inclusive' and 'disseminated', able to interest visitors of all ages and backgrounds in the local community and various local contexts.

To design innovative models of hospitality based on these principles has been the goal of a team of professors and researchers from the Politecnico di Milano. They aim to collect new, interesting case studies and, together with other partners, experiment with new hospitality solutions. The most interesting case studies and design experiments include 'horizontal hotels', 'short-term and long-term temporary hotels' and 'micro-architecture for hospitality in open spaces'.

INNOVATIVE MODELS OF HOSPITALITY: CASE STUDIES

Horizontal hotels

The most innovative hospitality model discovered during the Politecnico di Milano team's research in recent years is the so-called 'diffused hotel' or 'horizontal hotel'. Formally recognized only in 1998, when the region of Sardinia established it as an independent hotel category in its regional tourism law, the horizontal hotel is not in a single building but spread out over a territory (very often the historical city or village centre) among several buildings. It provides all the services of traditional hotels (reception, assistance, shared spaces, meals), but the rooms are scattered within a 200-metre radius of the historical centre and the hotel reception, shared spaces and restaurant. The rooms and/or apartments are set within palaces and apartments that are part of the historical centre and are expressions of the local culture. The scale of the hotel and the high level of integration

(from an architectural and social point of view) make guests feel like temporary residents of the area rather than traditional tourists.

'Horizontal hotels' permit cities and villages to restore and recuperate existing buildings, giving them new functions and a new life. In addition, this kind of activity stimulates existing and potential local entrepreneurs to create new businesses associated with new tourist demand, such as local gastronomy, arts and handicrafts (Dall'Ara 2009). This hospitality model is a sort of hybrid between bed and breakfast accommodation and traditional hotels.

Short-term and long-term temporary hotels

The Italian organization esterni, based in Milan and highly involved in the design of innovative ways of using public space, organized the first temporary house for filmmakers in 2004 (during the Milan Film Festival), followed in 2005 by the first temporary designers' house (during the Milan International Furniture Fair). In both cases (and at their subsequent editions), an unconventional space like an art gallery, an empty abandoned space, a university auditorium or a public market building was transformed for almost one week into a place where an international community of young creative people could meet, share experiences and stay for an affordable price.

Similarly, in Newcastle upon Tyne, Dott's Design Camp was organized in 2007. The project, led by Steve Messam, brought together teams of young designers and professionals, students, artists and architects from eight countries to develop sustainable tourism ideas. Participants examined urban camping, industrial heritage and agricultural tourism.

The concept of urban camping in particular was prototyped in order to experiment with a model for sustainable urban tourism. The design team transformed a disused space in Newcastle Gateshead into sustainable accommodation for visitors to the Dott 07 Festival in October 2007. In order to protect visitors from rain, the urban camp was based in an archway beneath Byker Bridge. The tents were located on platforms of varying heights in order to create a more urban environment (and to increase the density of the camp).

In the team's plan the area was to be electricity-free, with a common lounge, cooking and eating area to encourage sharing and conversation. Buses were to bring people from Central Station to the camp and recycled bikes were provided for Dott 07 visitors to explore the city.

The m-hotel, a recent concept designed by Tim Pyne Associates for London, is based on a different type of temporary hotel. The idea is to create a 'roving' hotel in vacant urban sites (especially car parks in emerging areas which the site owners are sitting on, waiting for land values to rise). The building consists of modules (each measuring 576 sq. ft) that slide into a steel frame; the outside is easily personalized (using bus-film technology) in order to contextualize

the building with respect to the specific site; construction materials and technologies make this prefabricated building easy to dismantle in the future (after 7 to 10 years).

Micro architecture for hospitality in open spaces

Aldo Cibic has recently developed *Microrealities*, a research programme presented for the first time at the International Architecture Exhibition of the Venice Biennale in 2004 and further developed through projects, exhibitions and workshops in collaboration with Italian and international schools of design (Politecnico di Milano and Domus Academy in Milan, the University Institute of Architecture in Venice (IUAV) and Tongji University in Shanghai).

The design research team has assumed the double task of inventing new strategies for everyday life and of suggesting new kinds of relationships with the habitat: the house, leisure spaces, workplace and public grounds. Alternative visions have been produced in which architecture is integrated with open spaces, services, infrastructure and objects. These 'visions' have the capability of capturing new responses to the vital needs of people living in major metropolitan centres, especially in suburbs and the places of greatest urban deprivation and social exclusion.

The main principles are:
– attention to small-scale architecture (micro-realities) and to small everyday situations, based on the idea that many

small situations, when combined, can generate larger, more significant stories;
– a search for new possible lifestyles that are simple, silent, with few objects, small spaces, in contact with nature and the changing seasons, and able to stimulate encounters, exchanges and sharing between people (residents and visitors);
– the design of new architecture, innovative services (meeting places, markets, playgrounds, etc.), products and furniture for daily living;
– localization in suburban areas with the aim of combining agriculture with residential villages;
– searching for sustainable beauty in the landscape and in the everyday lives of individuals (Cibic & Tozzi 2006).

The same attention to micro-scale living is expressed in *micro compact home [m-ch]*, a project developed by Professor Richard Horden of Munich Technical University (together with some colleagues from the same university, Horden Cherry Lee Architects, London, and Haack Hopfner Architekten, Munich): a lightweight, compact dwelling for one or two people within 2.6 m³. The product was first launched in Munich in November 2005 with the development of a case study village of seven micro-compact homes, sponsored by O2 company and built at Munich Technical University in order to accommodate six selected students and their British Professor. The micro-compact homes have all the necessary technological equipment and a high quality kitchen and bathroom (Slavid 2007.) Five of these prototypes were presented in the outdoor spaces of New York's Museum of Modern Art in the exhibition *Home Delivery: Fabricating the Modern Dwelling* (20 July-20 October 2008).

NEW DESIGN EXPERIMENTS

Urban design camping

Keywords emerging from the above mentioned case studies (like micro-scale, dissemination of elements, integration, outdoor experience, flexibility, temporary, etc.) were an important starting point for Milano Design Camping, a project developed for the Milan City Council by the team from Politecnico di Milano in collaboration with Triennale di Milano, organized by I Living, supported by Material Connexion Milan and Ferrino Spa, with the patronage of ADI, the Italian industrial design association, and the European association TensiNet. The project began in early 2009 with the aim of promoting new hospitality solutions in Milan, targeting young people interested in visiting the city throughout the year or for big events such as Milan Design Week (April) or Expo 2015.

Milan Design Camping aims include:
– to disseminate innovative and low cost hospitality ideas;
– to design and promote an international competition in order to collect innovative urban design camping ideas (January-June 2010, see www.designcamping.it);
– to disseminate the results of the competition through an exhibition;
– to establish a new urban design campsite in Milan for Expo 2015.

The core idea of hospitality in these initiatives is a new, sustainable and attractive model of camping, located in open urban spaces and characterized by flexibility of accommodation in relation to the number of visitors, and by a high level of integration between residents and guests, and between the site and the territorial context through the offer of advanced services and innovative cultural and social initiatives. Urban Design Camping is the term assigned to this new concept of hospitality based on the hybridization of the traditional idea of camping and a more urban and design-oriented approach where the settlement and units are in a city rather than in a natural landscape, and that accounts for the seasonal factor and the allure of an international design capital such as Milan, a high qualitative environment with advanced and sustainable facilities and services. The first activity was carried out during Milan Design Week 2009 (see figure 1). The Triennale di Milano and the central park of Milan (Parco Sempione) hosted an exhibition of innovative residential units for outdoor living, while inside the historical arena of Milan (located in the same park) three workshops and several seminars were organized by Politecnico di Milano. The first workshop, led by Massimo Duroni, focused on the design of single residential units with recycled materials (see figure 2); the second, carried out by Paola Trapani, addressed the design of vegetable gardens as a way to embellish the camp's open spaces and to bring local residents and guests into contact (see figure 3). The third workshop, coordinated by Peter Di Sabatino, sought new visions of a temporary urban camp

Figure 1: Workshop Design Camping: exhibition at the arena of Milan, April 2009.

based inside the arena in Milan (see figure 4). The results of these workshops were exhibited during Milano Design Week 2009 at the arena entrance. In November 2009 a further workshop with the title *Green village on the edge of the city*, leaded by Aldo Cibic and Tommaso

Figure 2: Workshop The sky over Milan, (workshop leader: Massimo Duroni), School of Design, Politecnico di Milano, April 2009.

Figure 3: Workshop Kitchen Gardening (workshop leader: Paola Trapani), School of Design, Politecnico di Milano, April 2009.

Figure 4: Workshop Camp.Mi (workshop leader: Peter Di Sabatino) School of Design, Politecnico di Milano, April 2009. Project by Paolo Matera, Giulia Minozzi, Daniele Pellizzoni, Anna Piccinelli.

Corà, was organized at the School of Design of Politecnico di Milano (see figures 5 - 7). The second activity relating to the international competition for the design of innovative

Figure 5: Workshop Green village on the edge of the city, School of Design, Politecnico di Milano, November 2009 (workshop leaders: Aldo Cibic and Tommaso Corà; scientific coordination: Luisa Collina). Project: Arcipelago. New neighbourhoods by: Francesco D'Onghia, Caterina Rosa, Silvia Sala, Ilaria Salvatore and Daria Svidir.

Figure 6: Workshop Green village on the edge of the city, School of Design, Politecnico di Milano, November 2009 (workshop leaders: Aldo Cibic and Tommaso Corà; scientific coordination: Luisa Collina). Project: Looking outside: in a corn field by: Michele Novello, Daniele Nobile, Antonio Prinzo, Diana Rizzoli and Laura Solvieri.

modules of urban camping was launched in early 2010. The camp envisaged by the competition consists of permanent units to host tourists throughout year and temporary elements (like tents) that can easily be provided to guests for a specific event and dismantled and repositioned as required, throughout the year. Additional space for tourists who bring their own tent or camper has not been envisaged at the present stage. The competition requires participants not only to

Figure 7: Workshop Green village on the edge of the city, School of Design, Politecnico di Milano, November 2009 (workshop leaders: Aldo Cibic and Tommaso Corà; scientific coordination: Luisa Collina). Project: Green camping by: Annalisa Lever, Denise Liguori, Hye Young Kim (KHAILY), Luca Cozzi, Amin Daneshgar, Lorenzo Bitto.

design the outside of the single unit, but also the interior with the necessary equipment.

CONCLUSION

Through these activities the Milan City Council aims to stimulate local and international designers and artists, the main target guests for the future camp, to help the city develop a new campsite model far removed from present ones designed for natural locations and not for urban environments: a place where sustainability matches aesthetics from the design of modules, products and furniture to the services that will be offered; where the visitor will feel like a guest and where the resident is given new opportunities to provide services to tourists; where a deep intercultural relationship between guests and hosts can take place; where the former are able to experience local sites and the latter to experience open and cosmopolitan ideas.

[1] Ezio Manzini, 'Culture of hospitality', Milan Design Camping Seminar, Milan, 21 April 2009.

AUTHORS / François Jégou and Stéphane Vincent

CHAPTER / Residencies in public institutions supporting local transition to sustainable ways of living

INTRODUCTION

The 27e Région[1] is a French public innovation laboratory based in Paris. It was created as a joint initiative of ARF[2], the national association of French regions and FING[3], a think tank focused on the use of information technologies for social change. The political objective of the 27e Région is to foster innovation and sustainability in public institutions, to renew regional policies and to test on a large scale, and within a network, new forms of territorial engineering and design. Still today, actions in the public area tend to be compartmentalized, preventing cross-fertilization between sectors and paradigmatical changes. The methods inherited from management, auditing, consulting and techno-economic innovation tend to demonstrate their inefficiency in the face of the increasing complexity and interdependence of environmental, climatic, social, economic, cultural and technological issues (Durance et al., 2008, Jouen 2009). Today public markets produce school buildings, services and public procedures that do not take users into account and even force them into ready-made solutions. Since its creation in 2008, the main activity of the 27e Région has been to promote *Territoires*

en Résidences, a series of *in vivo* innovation sessions settled in public institutions in French regions. Its core idea is inspired by long-term artist residencies in a particular context for the purpose of generating new projects in collaboration with the local population. The multidisciplinary team of *Territoires en Résidences* settles for three separate weeks over a four-month period in a college, health centre, neighbourhood digital services places or the regional council administration itself. Their goals are twofolds: to co-design with local stakeholders a future vision articulated in a set of long term scenarios, to implement a program of ready to start concrete short-medium term actions and projects targeting the future vision. Immersion, it appears, is one way of starting a healthy dialogue and encouraging stakeholders' capacity-building, development, ongoing progress and rapid prototyping of new public services.

The launch phase of *Territoires* is a programme of 15 different residencies over two years. Begun in early 2009, seven residences have successfully been completed and presented for mid-programme assessment in December 2009 at the French Regions Association

annual congress. These field experiences are still very fresh and require more time to analyse in order to firmly cement what has been learned: the residencies trigger great enthusiasm, boost energies and catalyse change but they are only the first step of the long-term transformation of the host institution and its innovation processes. But the variety of residencies experienced so far, the number of stakeholders involved in the field or as observers, and the positive feedback already received encourage a first tentative analysis of the process.

RESIDENCIES IN PUBLIC INSTITUTIONS AS A NEW MEAN OF REGIONAL INNOVATION

Residents were involved in a three-level research process: experimenting with participatory innovation via immersion with the local population; documenting each residency and feedback; and reorienting methodology. The *Resident Guide* and associated tool box (Figure 1) describes a partially guided flexible approach based on long periods of immersion in the host residence; a design-driven

Figure 1: Resident Guide presenting the state of the art of the residence methodology and process after one year of experimentation (photographs: François Jégou).

multidisciplinary creative team of three to four young designers, architects, sociologists, social entrepreneurs, or artists united by a design mindset; ethnographic-like observation and participative design techniques; self-orientation of the field work; co-design of the brief of the residence; iterative loop process between long-term vision and emblematic implementation, envisioning and simulation, experimentation and programming, etc.

The emerging *Territoires en Résidences* format is not new; it is part of a design approach to support social innovation in general (Jégou et al. 2009 and 2008; Manzini 2009, Mulgan 2006 and 2007, Thakara 2005) and situated participative innovation processes in particular (Leadbeater 2004, Dear Architect 2007). It has been here streamlined to adapt to multipurpose innovation in the public sector. It was conceived within the current attributes of the regions in France – education, health, transport, work, etc. – but can be applied in any kind of public institution, civil society organization, government body, or public service: city, urban agglomeration, neighbourhood, etc.

Beyond the character of localized innovation sessions and their apparent capability to trigger social change, we will take a broader perspective and consider a network of residences and their potential to engage the transformation of the territory at the regional scale. Our hypothesis here is that residences are a flexible and efficient format of innovation on the territory.

Based on the nature and experience of the few residences currently completed, we will try to show how this format addresses an intermediate level of experimentation deeply rooted in local contexts and territorial contexts. We will also try to imagine how a projected network of self-standing but connected residencies (experimentations) may generate a dynamic of territorial transformation via a relatively light and resilient process.

INNOVATION BETWEEN MACRO TOP-DOWN PROJECTS OF TERRITORIAL DEVELOPMENT AND MICRO BOTTOM-UP SOCIAL INITIATIVES

An intermediate level of innovation on the territory

Residences produce innovation processes rooted in the social fabric. Long periods of immersion make it possible to grasp the spirit of the place and to build trust with its inhabitants.

In Revin, Champagne-Ardennes Region, *Territoires en Résidences* settled in a college (Figure 2) and right away developed empathy and understanding with the local population, living among the degraded infrastructure of a 1970s working class neighbourhood and in a territory devastated by unemployment. The region has appropriated 38 million euros to build a brand new building based on plans displayed in the college entrance hall, but the project remains a question mark for everybody working there. As one regional manager said, 'We are building new hardware and we completely forgot the software...' The residence focused on connecting a social project with the

Figure 2: In Revin, Champagne-Ardennes Region, a new social project emerged from the residence: building an open campus as a resource for the surrounding territory (photographs: Matthew Marino, François Jégou).

architectural one, and on how can to interest the college population by catalysing various isolated initiatives into one social project in which they all believed. A future vision rapidly emerged from conversations: an open campus. A place that is not a burden for the territory

but a resource, open to the surrounding neighbourhood, to the city of Revin, and to nearby villages and territory. A dozen of projects have been consolidated during the period of residence, involving scholars in the promotion of local tourism, opening the college as a local conference hall for companies, organizing an annual fair for local NGOs, opening a new section teaching eco-construction, etc.

This example shows the clear potential of residences to be an intermediate level of innovation on the territory between macro top-down development and micro bottom-up initiatives: it starts with the local population, taking into account their concerns and engaging them to invent their own process of change. But the innovation process goes potentially far beyond the specific initiatives of a small group of social innovators. The population directly or indirectly includes scholars, professors, administrative and technical staff and their related families, more than 3,000 people... And the actions and projects are not only related to themselves but address the surrounding territory. The college's experience becomes a flagship for other colleges of the region (even before the social or infrastructural transformation has taken place) and induces a willingness in others to try similar experiences: in Tinqueux, in the same region, another residence has just begun and the emerging future vision is clearly aligned: a High Human Quality college[4]. The college, from a closed institution dedicated to teaching, emerges as a hub for local social initiatives.

Intermediation between grassroots initiatives and local governance

The intermediate level of innovation of *Territoires en Résidences*, beyond the dimension of the process on the territory, relates to the capabilities of intermediation between top-down and bottom-up they represent. In Rennes, in Bretagne, more than 1,600 residents are members of a local social digital network called La Ruche[5]. The network has been created and is animated by the NGO Bug where a residence settled. The initial motivation was to question the role of local social networks relative to the success of Facebook and Twitter. Individuals joined La Ruche more out of sympathy than to really use it, and though it claims many members, it doesn't seem to increase nor to develop real applications. An augmented citizenship proposed to use the local digital network to foster social initiatives and local change. It focuses on promoting La Ruche by connecting its members to the rest of the Rennes population and making

Figure 3. In Rennes, in Bretagne, the residence played an interesting role of intermediation, promoting projects between a grassroots local digital network and the town authorities (photographs: Jacky Foucher, Pierre Cahurel).

existing and potential applications visible in order to foster new ones. Initial ideas have appeared counter-intuitive at first: displaying the screen-prints of the digital map of La Ruche on public display; printing with ephemerous water jets process digital messages selected from La Ruche user dialogues to induce participation; installing signs inviting people to join La Ruche car pool stops (Figure 3). In addition to social network use to enhance local elective connectivity within the population, and the exploration of bridging modes between the digital and the physical to reduce the digital divide, residence results demonstrate an interesting capability of intermediation between grassroots initiatives and local governance. Within a three week period, very small dimension citizens initiatives were displayed on public space and accessed towns advertising panels, and local authorities were enabled to spot promising social initiatives and catalyse them. Residences seem to have a triggering effect and are an intermediate format of innovation to coordinate the bottom-up and the top-down, fostering innovation simultaneously at both levels, outlining solutions that spur social innovation and at the same time generating the appropriate framework that will enable their development.

A light real-size experimentation playing the role of a demonstrator

The overall financial and political costs of residences are relatively minor. Indirect social and infrastructure costs in case of failure are relatively low and limited to a localized mistakes

Figure 4: In Pionsat, in Auvergne, a residence activate strategic conversation between the local stakeholders to create a rural health centre (photographs: Julie Bernard, Marie Coirié).

compared in case of success to the potential benefits of both a real-size experimentation and the creation of a demonstrator. In Pionsat, a village in the vast, empty rural area of Auvergne, a residence has been organized to rethink the *Maison de Santé,* an initiative to maintain basic medical services in rural areas that lack doctors and medical infrastructure (Figure 4). But again, a new building doesn't solve the problem, neither in terms of attractiveness for young medical doctors nor of spontaneous adhesion from rural patients. The residence focuses on fostering dialogue. Many use cases allow improving mutual understanding between the different players. The residents settle on a bench during the

weekly street market to engage co-design with the population. Current doctors and local authorities collaborate with patients to imagine the *Maison de Santé* in terms of functionalities and related health services such as home care kits and travelling medical doctor equipment.

The *Maison de Santé* has begun to exist as a shared collective request of all different local stakeholders. The residence embodies the project before it starts and attracts political visibility as an experiment in progress. The residence is thus a simulation of the future partnership between stakeholders to implement the *Maison de Santé*. All this is achieved in a relatively short time and at low cost.

CONCLUSION

Residences seem to represent a light format of innovation (in time, money, risk, involvement) and they are intensely localized (based on field work and local participation). They don't require high level political decisions or involvement, are relatively short-term and recognized as being experiments. They address an intermediate level of innovation, are suited to the territory level, mediate between micro and macro levels, and become demonstrations of what could be: a concrete, sufficiently developed experiment with tangible results generated by ample participation. They can represent a significant step forward both in political terms and from project point of view.

A mosaic of tentative innovations

Residences represent a space where risk can be taken, where traditionally inertial and conservative public institutions can challenge routine processes, try innovative ideas and experience failure without fear. They maintain their experimental dimension throughout the process of transformation. Where the classical public development model is based on a small-scale pilot project followed by large-scale implementation, *Territoires en Résidences* resembles a succession of pilot projects, maintaining energy, freshness, and flexibility in the local context. It's an active learning and research process. At the territorial level, it's a molecular transition process based on the accumulation of local independent actions. Compared to burdensome territorial development based

on planning, failure of one residence doesn't endanger the whole territorial transition. The systemic level is reached progressively but not addressed at first sight: as already shown above, the Champagne-Ardennes Region is progressively exploring the college of tomorrow, not as a futuristic fixed brief but towards a permanent state of experimentation in all 80 regional colleges (Figure 5).

A network of local transformations in synergy

The residences are connected and subject to continuous mutual influence. Regular inter-residence meetings aim to improve the methodology but also to serve the meta-level of territory regional transition. Lessons learned are reported to the Association of the French Regions (ARF) for cross-fertilization. Within the same region, a programme of more residences will serve the strategic transformation of the territory. This scheme is currently being explored by the Nord-Pas de

Figure 5. Champagne-Ardennes regional authorities begin a residence in second secondary school in Tinqueux outlining the willingness to establish residences as a permanent renewal and stimulation process for all regional secondary schools (photographs: Gabi Farage, Olivier Bedu).

Calais Region: the Direction of Future Research and Sustainable Development is organizing a residence within a foresight exercise on suburban areas. This residence is meant to be the first of series to monitor critical needs and dynamize Regional Council policies.

Open questions and follow-up

Residences represent a potential format for fostering transformation at the territory level, a network of independent, localized innovation processes acting in synergy toward larger scale transformation of the territory. This transformation is based on a permanent state of interconnected experiments in order to ensure continuous questioning of the changing process and increased resilience.

This challenge will require exploring open questions at various levels, such as: How to deploy the model within regional public institutions and beyond its administrative rigidity? How to track or form the local human resources necessary to gather enough professional teams of residents? How to project a dynamic and reactive programme of residences as the result of a top-down territory strategy and bottom-up pertinent initiatives?

---

[1] The 27e Région is a French NGO based in Paris and funded by the Association of French Regions, the Caisse des Dépots and the European Commission.

[2] Association des Régions de France.

[3] Fondation Internet Nouvelles Générations.

[4] The French is Le lycée Haute Qualité Humaine, which is a play on HQE (Haute Qualité Environnementale), high sustainable quality a label applied to eco-construction.

[5] La Ruche translates as 'the hive' and is composed of bees, single participants and hives, local participating NGOs and institutions.

AUTHOR / Giampiero Pitisci

CHAPTER / Pedagogical tool kit to investigate social innovation in urban environments: the LOLA project

INTRODUCTION

This paper describes the LOLA project, launched in 2006 and developed by Strategic Design Scenarios, Brussels, and DIS Indaco, Politecnico di Milano, within the Consumer Citizen Network (CCN) and the Sustainable Everyday Project (SEP).

LOLA, which stands for Looking for Likely Alternatives, is a didactic tool to approach sustainability by investigating social innovation. It is an inquiry-based learning process conceived as an 'enabling tool kit' that assists teachers and students to identify, investigate and communicate examples of sustainable ways of living in their urban environment.

The LOLA project is one of the didactic follow-ups to the EMUDE (Emerging User Demand in Sustainable Solutions 2004-2006) research project, which involved design schools from eight European countries in a process of collecting examples of social innovation. For this project, the designers went beyond reflection on the eco-design of goods, and questioned larger systems related to everyday activities, focusing on

exploring new areas of social innovation and meeting the 'creative communities' who are promoting it. Discussions followed on how to turn this process into a didactic activity to raise awareness of sustainability issues through the investigation of examples of social innovation. Initially, LOLA's purpose was to provide a tool kit to secondary schools that enables teachers and pupils to create learning sessions. But it rapidly turned into a tool for a wider range of age groups, from the primary school to the university level. LOLA is neither a ready-to-use package nor a fixed exercise; as an educational tool kit it is meant to *stimulate*.

The entire Human Cities project stresses that our contemporary urban environment is the result of a complex interplay between layers of artefacts – from a micro- to macro-scale – services and users.

Some of these interplays are embedded in alternative places for promoting collaborative services and social cohesion. Examples include 'Jardin Nomade' in Paris, which acts

Figure1: Promising cases: loan gardens, Overhecht, The Netherlands: Residents helped by the municipality and a gardening association to take care of parcels of public gardens.

as neighbourhood connector: a group of people squat city wastelands to organize vegetable plots and collective activities around neighbourhood gardening; 'Aquarius' in Eindhoven, The Netherlands, a large garden for an elderly housing community sharing, collective spaces and organizing mutual help and support within the community; 'Loan Gardens', in Overhecht, The Netherlands, which maintains public green areas involving neighbourhood residents who imbue an area with an identity and interact socially; 'Neighbourhood Shares', The Hague, The Netherlands, where residents take responsibility from local authorities for certain neighbourhood

Figure 2: Promising cases: the Bracka Street Festival, Krakow, Poland: owners of shops in Bracka let people present what they have to offer.

maintenance tasks; and the 'Bracka Street Festival' in Krakow, Poland, where during a few days Bracka shop owners provide street light installations to help people presenting what they have to offer without requiring specific permission from public administration[1].

These very local initiatives are progressively reshaping parts of the city in unexpected ways. They comprise *enabling* solutions that mix objects, design capabilities and light architecture to restore relations of proximity,

Figure 3: Promising cases: Neighbourhood Shares, The Hague, Netherlands: Residents have taken responsibility from local authorities for certain maintenance tasks in their neighbourhood.

create meaningful bonds between individuals and favour the emergence of more sustainable social initiatives. The LOLA project intends to help students to investigate how these creative communities interact today with urban spaces.

LOLA: LOOKING FOR LIKELY ALTERNATIVES

As mentioned above, the LOLA project aims to focus pragmatically on day-to-day concerns

and the proximity of initiatives located in the neighbourhood. In effect, education for sustainability generally relates to abstract systems, complex interactions and big numbers. But how does one encourage children, students and adults to feel concerned about carbon emissions, water shortages and acid rain? They must be able to grasp these problems in a concrete fashion. LOLA seeks sustainable initiatives within walking distance of schools and universities, and people who invent new solutions in their daily lives that are likely to reduce their impact on the environment and to regenerate the social fabric. Radical change doesn't come only from top-down policies. LOLA proposes to focus on bottom-up initiatives, which don't require political decision-making or change at a global level before they can be implemented. It seeks initiatives that can be implemented by a small group of people who are creative and industrious enough to invent more sustainable ways of everyday living.

From a more pedagogical point of view, LOLA can be described as an investigation based on interviews. It doesn't require any particular knowledge or preparation for the teacher: students will learn together by asking questions, collecting material, wondering why and how the initiative they are investigating may have more or less impact on the environment. They will compare points of view, return to class having acquired their own local knowledge, and learn to live in a busy, evolving environment and permanently question it. LOLA emphasizes the student's participation, or *active learning*. But LOLA is not a means to pure discovery, since the investigation's purpose – finding

promising cases of social innovation – and expected results are not clearly framed. LOLA places the responsibility of learning on the learners: their exploration of their surroundings and reconciliation of contradictory explanations in interviews should trigger their curiosity and willingness to access more conceptual knowledge and understand the issues of sustainability.

LOLA promotes the idea that a school may become more efficient by opening up to the outside world; that schools are agents of social change. Beginning with concrete observations is likely to increase a student's motivation to learn about sustainability and lead him to discover in his own community how revised traditional practices and new forms of sustainable living can reduce negative environmental impact. It promotes a creative approach where teaching methods can evolve and new material can be added to suit different contexts in terms of age, location and time available. Finally, as sustainability is deeply rooted in a local context, what is a promising solution in one place might not be adapted to another. Beyond the variety of solutions each class might encounter in its investigations, LOLA proposes to share results, compare sustainable solutions observed by classes in different locations and progressively build an international repository of sustainable ways of living through its web platform (www.sustainable-everyday.net/lola).

LOLA's core process is articulated in five steps presented as a flexible set of cards that make it possible to customize and adapt

an exercise to any teaching situation. The core element of the LOLA tool kit is a set of so-called Step-by-step Cards that describe possible steps toward 1) identifying sustainable ways of living; 2) searching for a promising initiative; 3) investigating and contacting protagonists; 4) clearly documenting what they do; and 5) discussing investigation results. For each of these steps, each card proposes options, multiplying the number of possible ways to implement LOLA. The cards are large, with big titles and explicit drawings.

A Student Reporter Book is also included in the LOLA tool kit. It is the main investigation tool for students to organize their interviews, containing basic concepts and examples of initiatives to investigate; interview question guides and photograph checklists; progressive reporting formats to organize information and images, personal comments and disclosure agreements.

After the investigation, students are invited to set up an exhibition based on their selected initiative and discussion. *This exhibition material is a basic foundation to explain the process.* Starting material for an exhibition is also provided in the tool kit, and an Exhibition Guide suggests multiple ways of installing a low-cost exhibition. Its aim is to facilitate the diffusion of LOLA and to promote it at various levels, from a group of teachers at the same school or university to a teacher convention at a regional or national level.

For this purpose, LOLA 'ambassadors' have been established to promote it at national levels. Ambassadors coordinate LOLA

Figure 4: The LOLA Toolkit. Samples of the Exhibition Guide, the Brochure and pictures of a LOLA exhibition.

information dissemination and promotion within their countries. In particular, they collect feedback on implementation via feedback forms, to help the LOLA core team record all experiences and improve the LOLA tool kit.

The entire tool kit is downloadable for free from the LOLA website. All tool kit elements are an open source: they can be used for all purposes except commercial ones. The tool kit's core elements have been designed with less text and more graphics to facilitate translation (the Step-by-step Cards are already available in seven languages). Local LOLA teams of teachers are encouraged to open regional or national LOLA blogs in their own languages and promote their own improvements. A central blog has been created as a reference point for coordinating activities. The main process blog hosted communication

of shared interest and, by providing the possibility of leaving comments to every single posted article, it was seen as a catalyst for exchanging experiences between pilot project teams. Comments were seeds for discussion about the project's future development.

Various implementations of LOLA have taken place. They show a wide range of applications, from primary schools to universities, from long project periods to one-day events; from isolated initiatives to, for example, the attempt to officially adapt LOLA to the national curriculum in Ireland, where the process continues. In Brussels, the tool kit was used for a half-day event on environment and health; in Spain, 19- to 20-year-old students sought a local social initiative, documented it and then tried to reproduce it. In Latvia, more than 100 12- to 13-year-old students from ten schools were

involved in implementation. Thus LOLA is more of an 'enabling kit' than a mere 'teaching kit'.

Another remarkable LOLA process was implemented in Florianópolis, Brazil. In the second semester of the 2008 academic year, LOLA was inserted in the programme of Eco-design, a fifth semester course of the Graphic Design undergraduate degree programme at the Federal University of Santa Catarina (UFSC), in Florianópolis, State of Santa Catarina, Brazil. The course programme includes study of eco-design theories, which incorporate environmental aspects into product development. In a certain way, as Professor Gonçalves said, 'the use of LOLA caused an academic move from a theoretical to a practical approach'. The students already possessed some skills in other methodologies and were able to adjust parts of the LOLA tool kit to meet their needs and to face a new social and economic environment. Following that, LOLA was approached as whole, mainly through the presentation of the Step-by-step Cards, which were organized so students could get acquainted with the entire process and be prepared to use it. For this purpose, they had the possibility to browse a catalogue of promising social innovation cases available on the LOLA web platform. These cases were taken as references for academic debates, as well as models for future research. The students selected some initiatives and over two weeks conducted individual field investigations according to the Student Reporter Book. An upgrade was added to the process, since students should also note the potential use of design in the cases under investigation. As one student remarked, 'We generally use other methodologies of design...here, design was used as a tool of assistance for initiatives.'

Group findings and the role of design were debated, especially regarding the relevance of the latter to the development of creative communities. Two social entrepreneurs shared their experiences in the field of social innovation. Two weeks later the groups reported their design intervention proposals and a debate was launched in order to evaluate this first experience with LOLA. Overall, the activity involved three moderators (a professor, an assistant professor, and a student monitor) and 29 students, who performed the several phases of the process over nearly two months.

Three cases of sustainable social innovation in Florianópolis were identified and reinforced: an initiative conducted by the Community Council of Pantanal (CCPan), an association of local residents that organizes community social activities; 'Forest Park of Córrego Grande', an organization that promotes environmental education courses and park tours; 'Natural Products Fair', which offers local organic products. For all three initiatives, students proposed several designs to improve their efficiency.

This experience resulted in the identification in their own neighbourhoods of cases that previously went unnoticed by the students. In addition, the confrontation of theoretical and practical aspects also dealt with important concepts for eco-design, such as social innovation, sustainability, creative communities and collaborative organizations, which are not a priority in any typical design programme. Potential design interventions were identified and projects were sketched regarding such possibilities.

A summary of this experience with LOLA was presented at SEPEX – the Week of Education, Research and Extension of the Federal University of Santa Catarina – an official event in its seventh year. It attracted almost 50,000 people from the academic community, Santa Catarina public schools and the general public.

CONCLUSION

This brief description has tried to describe how the LOLA project seeks to foster positive attitudes and behaviour towards social innovation and sustainable lifestyles, and how it represents a promising methodology to investigate social innovation within public spaces. The next years for LOLA are likely to be intense: fully integrated in PERL (the Partnership for Education and Research about Responsible Living, funded by the Consumer Citizenship Network (CCN) and financed by UNEP/UNESCO; see www.hihm.no/concit), LOLA will enter a new phase of development and improvement. Alongside already existing implementations, LOLA hopes to solidify its implementation in national curricula, such as those of Latvia and Ireland, and in the CSPE (Civic, Social and Political Education) curriculum.

[1] For more details, see A Meroni, Creative Communities. People inventing sustainable ways of living, Edizioni POLI Design, Milan, 2007.

AUTHOR / Serena Pollastri

CHAPTER / **Volunteered geography as a driver for community-based services**

INTRODUCTION: THE RISE OF COLLABORATIVE SERVICES ON A DIGITAL PLATFORM

The diffusion of the Internet has been made possible by innovations in Information Technology and infrastructure. Its use has quickly spread, making the Internet the most important platform for exchanging and publishing any kind of information.

In 2004 an important revolution in the user's role occurred. This was mentioned for the first time by O'Reilly (2005) when he described the progression from what he called Web 1.0, where the Internet was a tool for spreading information in a unidirectional relation with the user, to Web 2.0, which allows users to participate in the process of content generation.

This revolution, together with the massive diffusion of Internet, formed the basis for a huge process of social innovation. New tools for collaboration are emerging thanks to the diffusion of peer to peer systems and open networks where innovations and content quality and heterogeneity are provided by a networking system of collaborative services on digital platforms. Web 2.0 platforms are created from the contributions, stories and identities of users who can look up, comment, and sometimes modify content generated by others.

All this means that collective platforms are now meeting points for individuals from different realities. This calls for a new definition of community. In addition to the traditional idea of community as a group of people living in the same geographical location, we must now consider communities of people who share the same values and social identity, though they may live very far apart.

A DIFFERENT GEOGRAPHY FOR COMMUNITY NARRATION

Thanks to technical improvement in the field of data representation, maps have become one of the preferred tools for geographically distributed data visualization.

In much of the data stored in digital platforms localization is a crucial aspect that can determine the relevance of the information itself. Moreover, in some user-generated content platforms the quality of contributions depends on the knowledge the contributor has of the place where they are located.

A new, democratic, concept of geography is becoming more popular, where a map is no longer a closed and prescriptive representation of space but an open table to which anyone can add his own representation of the territory. According to Farinelli (2003), the world is a collection of political, social, economical and cultural relations characterizing human life. That's why the apparent simplicity of cartography, used to represent the earth, hides a complexity that opens new narrative possibilities.

These opportunities have been explored by different artistic and philosophic movements in the 20th century. From the Dada experience, to the urban wanderings promoted by Debord and the situationists (1958), to the contemporary experiences of emotional geography (like the 'San Francisco Emotional Map', by Nold, or the 'Real Time' project in Amsterdam), different territorial maps have been created, each telling a story and giving a new subjective vision of the territory. As will be explained in the following paragraph, the task of new ICT in this context has been to make the collaborative process possible, facilitating interaction with the GIS (Geographic Information System) and integrating different contributions on a single thematic table that shows a multifaceted vision of a space.

Interest in maps in the context of service design is not related to the infographics itself, or to the kind of data mapped. The map acts as a service driver where the information stored, or the way it is built up, becomes an organizational element with a specific aim that goes beyond the on-line interaction of the people generating, updating and consulting it. In some contexts, in fact, the map can become an aggregating tool for a group, driving particular actions in the physical world and interactions between members.

The map, as a shared tool, encourages the so called cosmopolitan localism (Manzini 2005) that integrates the local into a global framework. The phenomenon of globalization, and the rise of networking, have given a new importance to the local dimension, creating a new sense of place, which is no longer an isolated reality, but a node of a globally diffused net.

Granovetter (1973) has categorized interpersonal ties as strong, weak or absent. People bound by a strong tie tend to interact with each other, making information circulate. Weak ties, on the other hand, exist among people who are not closely connected

Figure 1: Maps for service design.

but are members of an open network in which information is diffused rather than transmitted. According to Granovetter, such ties are 'the channels through which socially distant ideas, influences, or information' can reach an individual.

In this sense the map spreads in two ways: one connecting the local to the global through weak ties, and the second through strong ties, connecting members of the community that creates the information on the map and to which the map refers.

the map becomes service driver when the interaction user-map -user generates connections among communities and/or individuals in the real world

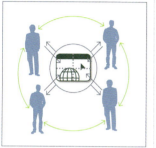
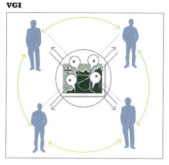

Figure 2: From traditional maps to VGI.

Figure 3: Graphic elaboration from Open Street Map.

Services created on these assumptions can be very heterogeneous, following the typologies of contents mapped and the kind of possible interaction among people.

COLLABORATIVE MAPS FOR SERVICE DESIGN

A GIS is a computer-based information system that captures, stores, edits, analyses, shares and displays geographical information. Technically, a GIS includes a set of applications to integrate different kinds of spatial data, which can be combined to obtain new derived information.

In recent years a set of innovations in the field of GIS have made possible the birth and spread of a phenomenon known as Volunteered Geographic Information (VGI). This neologism, created by Goodchild (2007), is used to define the practice of using Web tools to create, edit and share geographical information voluntarily produced by individuals. VGI can be considered a special case in the more general scenario of user-generated contents on the Web and collaboration on digital platforms (see figure 2). The most compelling example of the phenomenon is probably that of Google Maps and Google Earth, developed in 2005[1]. In these new products, some of the straightforward capabilities of GIS have

been opened to the public, democratizing the process of information mash-up, which is 'the ability to superimpose graphic information from sources distributed over the Web, many of them created by amateurs' (Goodchild 2007).

From that moment the so-called process of GIS Wikification, the Web-based mass participation in VGI (Sui 2008) began, and a large number of collaborative digital services based on the spatial localization of information have been created.

It is crucial, at this stage, to mention and explain the potentiality of open geospatial data. The concept of free geography is promoted by the international association OSGeo (Open Source Geospatial Foundation, www.osgeo.org), created to support open source geospatial software, free maps and the collaborative development of community-led projects in the field of geography. One of the projects supported by OSGeo is OpenStreetMap (www.openstreetmap.org), which is a free, editable map of the world, created and updated by the community. The fact that the map is free means that it can be used for basically any purpose, can be printed, embedded in a blog or website, and, if needed, bugs and errors can be corrected (see figure 3).

From the OSGeo platform, several kinds of free software can be downloaded, and the code can be personalized according to the project's specific needs.

The value of the winning combination of OpenStreetMap with OSGeo free software in the process of service design is the possibility for in-depth design of the interaction, according to the specific characteristics of the service and the end-user community.

A designed service based on community maps normally includes a basic map (open or closed depending on how crucial the role of the map itself is[2]), a set of layers applied to the map for information mash-ups, and an on-line user-accessible digital platform that stores the contributions of the community and allows different layers of interaction (from map navigation and editing to community activities).

Following the Granovetter model combination of weak and strong ties, the winning user composition for a service like this includes both individual users and communities. Simplifying Granovetter's concept, we can consider members of a single community as connected by strong ties and members of different communities or groups as connected by weak ties. In the first case, the strength of the service is that by allowing the circulation of information among members and reinforcing group ties, it can help the visualization of 'site-specific' topics, generate actions and create a more intense sense of belonging. With the diffusion of information along weak ties, it is likely that different communities will start to interact, stimulated by their common interest in certain topics. Finally, the possibility of interaction by members from different

Sanoodi

Open Flights Map

open source activity

National Weather Service

Figure 4: Examples of the use of Open Layers.

Figure 5: Miro Web page; "Stories from the city".

communities, using the platform to know more about different realities, cannot be excluded.

Because the quality of the map increases with the number and heterogeneity of contributions, it is important to make the service as inclusive as possible[3], designing, when necessary, a way to solve the digital divide, for example, for the elderly, children, or poor people.

STEPS OF THE PROCESS AND THE MIRO CASE STUDY

The first step in designing a service based on a collaborative map is necessarily to acquire a deep understanding of the characteristics of the community to which the service is addressed. For example, an association called Izmo has

developed 'Insinto', a method aimed at building participatory knowledge of an urban area (insito.izmo.com). They promoted workshops to collect information (events, opinions, memories) provided by inhabitants of a certain area; all the data is localized in an interactive map on a web platform based on 'wiki' technology. The aim of this case study is understanding the community, in order to transmit it to those who are interested in the development of the area or in planning activities.

Another crucial step is to identify the digital tools to build the map and the platform. In the previous paragraph the criteria for selecting the kind of map and information mash-up software were mentioned. Similar attention has to be paid to the platform: user interaction with the map, the community and the website in general should be easy and focused on the service objectives. Nevertheless, in some cases, in order to stress the inclusiveness and visibility of the service and keep a lower investment, a good compromise might be to rely on existing popular social networks and blog platforms.

Since the digital platform is the infrastructure of the service, which manages information and communication flows, it is also the part of the system that enables the transformation of Web-based interaction into definite actions in the real world.

This passage is sometimes just a natural evolution of the online interaction of the user to achieve his objectives in the service, without the use of any other element external to the platform; in other cases, in order to

upgrade the system from an online social network to a collaborative service, it is also important to design a set of enabling solutions (Manzini 2005) that make the action or the connection of individual users or communities in the real world possible.

The Miro case will now be examined in depth in order to have a complete view of the main characteristics of such a service.

The intuition that has driven the development of the Miro project is that each inhabitant of a certain city (in this case Milan) has its own experience of the territory. By putting all the visions produced by a large and heterogeneous group of users together on a map, a giant collage representing the inner diversity of local reality will be created: a kind of 'participated image' of the city. When this map is shared it becomes a tool both to help residents explore the area where they live in greater depth, discovering interesting unknown realities, and for travellers, who can use it as an unconventional travel guide, entering in contact with the place they want to visit thanks to the contributions of the local community.

Basically, Miro consists of a Web-based platform, where the map of Milan is embedded and produced by OpenStreetMap. On this map, layers of shared information able to connect inhabitants and travellers are created using the free software OpenLayers, promoted by OSGeo. The first layer, called 'Stories from the City', groups all the contributions about places that characterize the daily life of the contributors, and extraordinary things they find in the city;

subcategories are special places, events, food, shops, culture, nightlife (see figure 5). Tourists can navigate the map, select meaningful information, mark it as favourite and use it to create a printable personal travel guide.

Members of the local community can participate more profoundly in the service by deciding to become *hosts*. In this case, they can mark their house on the map, and specify the characteristics of the hospitality they want to offer to travellers.

Tourists who decide to become *guests* can navigate the layer of the map called 'Open Doors', which is the interactive representation of all the available accommodation offered by the hosts. Once the connection is created, the guest can decide to subscribe to a journey.

After the guest has paid a low fee, the host receives validation of the identity of his prospective guest plus a basic kit to support the hospitality. Money paid by travellers is used towards funding service costs, while the hospitality itself is offered for free.

Nevertheless, it is important to reward the participation of users, giving value to their contributions. This happens thanks to the collaboration of shopkeepers and

associations in the service. They can mark their activities on the map and keep a personal page with various information, providing gift certificates or services in return.

Every contribution by the user is measured in 'points' that can be collected (higher values in points are given to the hospitality offers); by reaching different goals the user can access prizes offered by commercial activities and associations.

The three main groups of actors, helped by service promoters, collaborate in the generation of a deeper knowledge of local reality, where diversity is a quality and the exchange of experiences is a consequence.

CONCLUSION

A community using a map to show different visions of the same space on a common table can help the integration of different coexisting realities, transcending prejudices and distrust, promoting a deeper knowledge of the territory and reinforcing the sense of belonging to a community. The use of ICT can increase service accessibility, enhancing communication between different, geographically distant communities.

That's why services based on community-generated maps represent promising systems to facilitate the sustainable development of local realities, like nodes of a net, each with a clear, multifaceted identity.

---

[1] In 2004, Google acquired a company called Keyhole Inc. that developed a product called Earth Viewer, renamed Google Earth in 2005.

[2] Since it normally takes a lot of work to build ex-novo the whole structure, a list of priorities has to be made in order to decide if it is better to adopt a close but customizable map, or an open map with tailored open source software.

[3] Of course, for some kinds of maps, for example, those with a scientific purpose, the inclusiveness of the service, and the way different members can contribute, has to be controlled.

AUTHORS / Rafaella Houlstan-Hasaerts and Nicolas Malevé

CHAPTER / Cartography as a common good

CARTOGRAPHY IN QUESTION

Cartography and power are closely related: who controls the map controls the territory, and this is true at several levels. The person who consults it, insofar as he knows how to interpret it, gains the ability to identify his position in space. The person who creates it – who is situated one step above – proposes (or imposes) his vision of the territory, as he perceives or projects it. The person who possesses it, finally, decides how to distribute it and consequently to grant or deny others the power he has concerning the territory. In fact, a map is hardly a harmless tool: figurative as well as projective, a simulation of space as much as a space for simulation, it is found at the very source of military strategies, mercantile capitalism, territorial divisions and symbolic domination (Lacoste 1976; Monmonier 2002). In the particular case of cities, it has determined by and large what is to be drawn and measured, and consequently, what is to be built or at least planned. Cartography, formerly reserved strictly to a minority, is now opening up to a broad range of users. With our greater mobility, as neo-nomads in a global world, we use and find them everywhere: in public transport, tour guides, streets, shopping malls and on our computer screens or GPS. With Google Earth, Google Maps, Mappy and other geoportals, the whole world is offered on our computer screens in just a few clicks, free from any constraints with regard to scale and paper.

Pleased as one must be with this democratization of access to cartography, there are still some weak points. The first concerns the codes that have been imposed over the centuries in mapmaking that offer a unilateral vision of space. Indeed, today's complex and shifting territories seem to need representations that go far beyond a simple zenithal perception and conventions that tend to show space exclusively in terms of surface areas. Here is an example that is pertinent today: more than half the world's population lives in cities and many studies predict that this trend will intensify in decades to come. Consequently, there are serious reasons to think that the 21st century will be more urban than any other. But traditional – topographical – mapping essentially emphasizes square metres, showing a majority of huge, relatively unpopulated areas on a worldwide scale (oceans, countryside), and therefore it totally misses the urban phenomenon whose importance is not directly proportional to its size. Topographical cartography can also be questioned when it comes to representing contemporary urban living: city limits have become hazy – well-defined borders no longer exist and cities are no longer understood in opposition to nature. They no longer seem to be closed, limited entities – they move, expand, change from day to day, mocking the immobility of a map. In addition, the pre-eminence of a visual, two-dimensional representation of the city tends to make us forget that it is first and foremost a 'lived in' space, and our perception goes beyond that which is visible – a city can also be travelled, heard, felt, imagined. 'Despite its formidable power of abstraction, the limits of the map as we know it lie in the fact that often it only takes account of geometric, material, incorporated, objectified or abstract visions of the city, thus ignoring its cultural, sensitive and imaginative dimensions and clouding the scale of the places we live in, the way they interweave and overlap, denying or giving only a normative picture of social reality' (Avitabile 2004: 28). Moreover, beyond this questionable hegemony, this characteristic of representation on maps becomes even more problematic when 'the people who use them think they are true, although or because they are geometrical' (Lefebvre 1974: 417). Indeed, the concept of urban living in general and public space in particular has been – and still is – determined for the most part by officials, who mainly use administrative maps, statistics and administrative limits, without taking into account other visions of the city, particularly those of everyone who lives there on a daily basis.

To help improve this state of affairs, drafting and distributing maps should not be the privilege of some, but the right of everyone. However, tools that enable the community to create and distribute its own maps are still marginal. Of course, many cartographic services present on the Web go beyond simple consultation, and enable users to add to the content of maps and share them with other users. But this broader possibility is still only partial: most of this cartographic software is proprietary, their geospatial data are protected, and most of the resulting maps are subject to very strict conditions for use and distribution.

TOWARDS A SUBJECTIVE COLLECTIVE CARTOGRAPHY

For more than three years, a group in Brussels has been working on the *Towards a Subjective Collective Cartography* project[1]. This is an effort to see mapmaking – the maps themselves, the process of drafting them and the data associated with them – as a common good, in terms of access (universal rather than restricted), regulation (permissive rather than restrictive) and ownership (public rather than private). This desire to defend the right of the community to consult, create, publish and exchange maps, and have access to cartographic data, is both poetic and political. Poetic because it responds to the inevitable share of subjectivity in an approach to the territory and considers that multiple cartographic visions are as many possible metaphors of the world we live in. Political because it gives users the power to think individually or collectively about the territory and perhaps to influence its future. In the past, urban action could take place without or even counter to many users of the city, or occasionally with them in a sort of concession won over from or generously granted by the authorities, but things should be very different today. In fact, the way people feel about and perceive a city – and a map can be used to represent this – should be the keystone of the democratic decision-making process concerning the territory in general and public space in particular (Geddes 1915; Blondiaux 1999, 2008).

Given these observations and objectives, the *Towards*[2] project focuses on creating two different tools that are nevertheless complementary: an *Atlas of Brussels* on one hand that includes the various maps of the city (imaginary, anecdotal, emotional, etc.) and, on the other, a cartographic software project – *Tresor* – that will make it possible to create, consult, compare, and adjust the parameters that define maps, and complete, publish or use them as part of personal or collective projects. Over the last three years, various workshops have been organized in collaboration with artists, activists, urban planners, architects, graphic artists, computer programmers, etc., to set up these tools.

ABOUT THE PROCESS

Today, this *Atlas of Brussels* includes some 50 maps made by artists, activists, members of associative or academic circles, citizens, etc. These maps can be consulted online on the project's website. For website visitors (more than 100 unique visitors a day), the *Atlas* provides the occasion to consult various points of view on the city of Brussels, and understand how the different subjectivities emphasize particular aspects of public space.

And how does *Tresor* work? It doesn't work, per se, rather it 'puts to work'. During the workshops, participants asked themselves what elements cartographic software might include. Is it an interface with buttons, that produces a manipulation of symbols? Or is it something broader, encompassing a different way of going about things, negotiating with others, and another way of thinking about what using a computer could be? So when a group of people starts thinking, writing and talking about what this software might be, the software is already at work – the software puts the group to work. Of course, there is still a long way to go to reach something that can be used as a tool, but what is gained by using a ready-made tool? Would that be user-friendly or rather… user-deadly? The options in prefab software reproduce separations that are meaningless for

Figure 1: Atlas interface (screenshot: Constant vzw).

users, particularly those who took part in the cartographic workshops. For example, these tools separate artistic and technical functions, 'real' geography and drawing. Cartographic software no doubt allows a change in colours and icons here and there, but the organizational graphic principle is always the same, and this is of little interest, for example, to people who want to represent their neighbourhood in the form of a galaxy with planets and their relations in the form of a trail in the Milky Way. If they want to represent this map in an imaginary form,

they have to use graphic software, meaning that they lose any connection with geography. If, on the contrary, they use a GIS, they will have to give up their imagination. *Tresor* is the tool that refuses this segregation. There are no acceptable reasons for this division that springs from segmentation of the market and division of tasks in the economy – and there is nothing to prevent developing this kind of tool. Nothing? Of course there is: the fact that the people who are actually involved have interiorized this division themselves: I am an artist, so I draw; I am a map maker, so I measure things. The first effect of *Tresor*, before a single line of code had been written, was to break down mental barriers that had been internalized by participants.

In the second stage, the participants wondered about the possibilities for developing a tool that corresponds to the concept of 'common good' in terms of accessibility, regulation and ownership. These questions naturally led to the conclusion that the components of *Tresor* should be distributed in keeping with the principles governing free licences. In fact, in the case of a free licence, the authors of software or a visual or literary work authorize anyone to use, modify and distribute their creations, but with the restriction that they cite their sources and the previous authors, and that they redistribute their own derivative works using that same licence, under the same conditions. These free licences are more than just a simple, pragmatic solution used here and there. They are also rather like an internal constitution for joint projects that tries to ensure that public good stays public. The use of this type of licence is important at two levels

for *Tresor*. First, it simplifies exchanges between various users when producing maps: everyone has the right to reuse, modify, or comment on everyone else's creations and to produce other versions of these maps. Second, all the people who feel an affinity with this tool can correct, improve, test, document, translate it, etc.

In the third stage, participants realized that there was already a whole series of isolated free software programs (for example, software that can connect GIS databases, vector graphics software, etc.) that could offer many possibilities for mapmaking when put together in a network. The result is that *Tresor* is not a software programme as such, but a whole series of paths between existing free software programs, and a link for programs that do not communicate with each other. By means of a series of scripts, user strategies, plug-ins and add-ons, these existing software programs are incorporated into *Tresor* as the need arises. Each mapmaking project corresponds to a documented experiment, a published code and tested tools that fill the toolbox little by little. In this project, the first lines of code that were written created a connection between Inkscape[3], an open source programme for vector graphics and Mapserver,[4] a web-based map server, or Spip[5], a software for publishing articles on the web to create a timeline. More ambitious projects followed, such as Genderartnet[6], a map of female artists who are working in Europe or using Europe as a subject, and Busboitescartesmap[7] (BBCM), a sound map exploring the city of Brussels.

Figure 2: Interface snapshot, the software captures the audio fragments recorded near the post boxes.

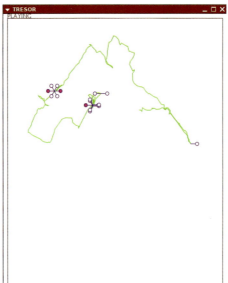

Figure 3: Interface snapshot, the user can filter the sounds and select the walks (screenshot: Constant vzw).

This last project gives an idea of the way the tool and the practices can be used together to explore and represent the territory in a different way. This project proceeds by means of sessions. A series of places are chosen for each session. These places correspond to post boxes in the city centre. They offer a large diversity of environments: they are near schools or major roads, in alleys, parks, etc. A group of participants goes to the city centre with a sound recorder and a GPS and visits the places that have been chosen. The clocks on the GPS and the recorder are

synchronized. When the participants get back, a software programme in the *Tresor* tool box extracts the audio segments corresponding to the location of the post boxes by comparing the time codes on the two appliances.

These audio tracks are then plotted on an interactive map so that people can listen to the cacophony of all the sounds recorded or choose only the sounds recorded in a specific place, and listen to one sample after another, or to the overall atmosphere of a location at different times of day.

As the participants are encouraged to vary the context of the place that they record (they can drum on the post boxes, or use them like an echo chamber; they can play with the sounds in the vicinity, or describe the environment or simply talk to each other), the sounds produced disclose new characteristics of urban space and invite everyone to continue his/her exploration of the town.

ONE THING LEADING TO ANOTHER

Even in its embryonic form, *Tresor* has been used as a software base for different cultural or artistic mapping projects, whether within the *Towards* framework or in other contexts. These first experiments using *Tresor* show that this type of tool, which adjusts to the user's needs rather than formatting them, can be truly useful to produce new and multifaceted representations of the territory. The next step will be to reach a broader audience (users of all kinds but also public authorities) so that, insofar as possible and necessary, the tool box helps generate real political and spatial transformations. That wish is about to be partially fulfilled. Some members of *Towards* have been asked by the Brussels 'Buildmaster' advising office to think about a way to gather various maps (administrative, subjective, etc.) of the Brussels Region in one interface, in order to facilitate territorial decision-making and public space design. Indeed, the mission of the 'Buildmaster' office is to develop a long-term vision for the Brussels Region, in consultation with public

Figure 4: A participant listening to the echo of a post box (photo: Constant vzw).

administrations and relevant external parties, and to contribute towards policy preparation and the execution of architectural strategies. The final aim of its mission is to create a high quality architectural environment (buildings, infrastructure, public space) in the Brussels Region. For the 'Buildmaster' office, one way to reach this quality is taking into account a multiscale and plural vision of the city, and gathering maps may help to achieve it. Thus, some members of *Towards* are working on the creation of this huge map interface of Brussels, using, among others, the *Tresor* tool box.

[1] The Towards a Subjective Collective Cartography project is an initiative of the not-for-profit organizations Recyclart, City Mine(d), Constant and the graphic designers from Speculoos, all based in Brussels. For further information see the following websites consulted 8 March 2010: Towards a Subjective Collective Cartography, www.towards.be; Recyclart, www.recyclart.be; City Mine(d), www.citymined.org; Constant vzw, www.constantvzw.org; Speculoos sprl, www.speculoos.com.

[2] Heretofore, the Towards project.

[3] Inkscape: draw freely, consulted 8 March 2010, <http://www.inkscape.org/>.

[4] Mapserver: open source Web mapping, consulted 8 March 2010, <http://mapserver.org/>.

[5] Spip, consulted 8 March 2010, <http://www.spip.net>.

[6] GenderArtNet, consulted 8 March 2010, <http://www.genderartnet.eu/>.

[7] Towards a Subjective Collective Cartography, Busboîtescartesmaps, consulted 8 March 2010, <http://www.towards.be/busboitescartesmaps/>.

II. / PLACE FOR PUBLIC

HUMAN CITIES / Place for public

Barbara Goličnik Marušić
and Matej Nikšič

USERS AS KEY ELEMENTS OF PUBLIC PLACES

Public spaces are among the formative entities of towns and cities. Examined either individually or as a network, they attract the interest of social science researchers and urban designers. Therefore, it is in the public interest for researchers and designers to join forces and inform each other so that designed public places are appreciated and user-friendly.

But this is nothing new. Five hundred years ago Shakespeare addressed this inseparable duality in one of his dramas, asking, 'What is the Citie, but the People? True, the People are the Citie' (Coriolanus, act 3, scene 1). At roughly the same time, although not referring directly to people and places but seeing people as playing a key role, the multitalented thinker, artist, scientist and engineer Leonardo da Vinci held that 'man is the measure of the universe'. The many theoretical and practical works reflect the incessant search for and debate over the importance of the person as a crucial element in urban design. They vary in their popularity, approaches, findings, and final practical usefulness and implementation. Accordingly, there have been discussions about space as a physical phenomenon, a state of mind, an entity with an identity, or a product of social processes.

Usually, urban designers, architects and landscape architects are quite concerned about creating attractive settings where people can live, work and play. However, although practical and pragmatic, their work has not always been as deeply rooted as it could be in the theoretical and empirical work of social science researchers such as philosophers or psychologists. This is now changing and affecting design rather slowly. Surely, seeking an attractive and visually pleasing spatial composition is a very important part of the design process. But at the same time, designers have a responsibility to create places for a broad spectrum of users, thus it is necessary to aim to aspire to a high level of artistic composition with the potential to host a wide array of uses. A pleasing layout with basic equipment is not enough.

Within these endeavours some specific fields of work and initiatives developed that put the users first. They do not only reflect the needs and aspirations of definite groups of users but also indicate the shift towards better places to live in general. For example, along with the enormous rise of the pressure of motorised traffic onto the open public urban space non-motorised users of public spaces, such as pedestrians, started to be given more attention (Morgan 1996), the rise of the awareness of the needs of the specific groups of people gave rise to the inclusive urban design (Preiser & Ostoff 2001). Besides, the sustainability issues exposed also the fact that humans are not the only users of urban space; they share it with other beings having their own demands and specific needs (Wheater 1999). Also, the concept of loose spaces and their role in urban design and urban life (Frank & Stevens 2007) is recognised as valuable, especially as expression of place identity and peoples' attachment to their neighbourhood or area.

The book's second part, 'Place for public', thus addresses the design of places such as parks and squares in city centres, and approaches that might improve design to better serve its various and diverse users. The first chapter, *Urban play and recreation: exploring a comprehensive vision for the future in urban recreation in New York,* by Miodrag Mitrasinović, Scott G. Pobiner and Eduardo

Stazsowski, reveals approaches developed at the Parsons School of Design Strategies that explore the relationship between urban play and recreational practices and help authorities in planning and decision-making. The second chapter, *Designing an urban park as a contemporary user-friendly place,* by Ina Šuklje Erjavec, shows the process of developing a medium-sized city park in the centre of Ljubljana. The third and fourth chapters focus on empirical data related to users in places. Barbara Goličnik Marušić's *Designing public places with users in mind* debates behaviour-mapping as a tool and maps as scripts of empirical knowledge that might provide insight to user-patterns and usage-spatial relationships that are often not obvious at first glance. Similarly, Matej Nikšič's chapter *Mapping a perceptual dimension of open urban public space* highlights a mapping technique for gathering another type of soft information about usage-spatial relationships.

He comments on the user's perception of visual qualities of places and their possible influences on design and decision-making in the design process. The chapter, *Regeneration of historic sites in the city centre of Ljubljana: the role of public participation in public space design,* by Biba Tominc, Nina Goršič and Breda Mihelič, addresses historical sites in cities and resident participation in neighbourhood regeneration and improvement, focusing on the local park and inner courtyards. And *Supporting local participation: lessons from the PoLok project* by Marko Peterlin and Aidan Cerar discusses the role of local residents in public space conception and design process in a broader context of Slovenia.

Part Two pays greater attention to actual users in places and searches for options how to negotiate spatial forms regarding user needs and habits, place perception, place engagement and expectations. In addition, from a

methodological perspective, Part Two promotes GIS as
an effective practical tool to build, develop and maintain a
body of empirical knowledge using interactive behaviour
maps as its scripts (Goličnik Marušić), mental maps of
either individual or common images of perceived areas
(Nikšič), and a comprehensive system for regeneration
of selected areas (Tominc, Goršič and Mihelič). To
implement such knowledge in urban public open space
design, research findings must be brought to bear
on decision-making, evaluation and management.

AUTHORS / Miodrag Mitrasinović, Scott G. Pobiner and Eduardo Staszowski

CHAPTER / Urban Play and Recreation:
Exploring a Comprehensive Vision for the Future of
Urban Recreation in New York City

INTRODUCTION

The Urban Play and Recreation course explores relationships between urban play, public space, and recreational practices in New York City. In order to explore these relationships in real-life situations and to develop realistic scenarios for alternative approaches to urban recreation, School of Design Strategies partnered with the New York City Department of Parks and Recreation (NYCPRD) in 2008. Our initial conversations with our partners revealed an opportunity to initiate a multi-year project that would create opportunities for knowledge-building and exchange among scholars and practitioners. Parsons faculty and students have the unique opportunity to learn from – and work with – the Department of Parks and Recreation, as well as learn from the broad network of their other partners. We envision the exchange to take place through studios, critical theory studios, and ongoing faculty research in areas such as participatory design, sustainable social innovation, urban studies, public space and game design. The breadth that Parsons brings to this kind of partnership is unique in its capacity to incorporate a diverse range of interests and domains of design expertise.

The purpose for this complex and ongoing project is to create a comprehensive new vision for 21st-century urban recreation in NYC. During the 2009 spring semester, the first phase of this project was also joined by two of the NYCPRD's not-for-profit partner organizations, Hester Street Collaborative and Partnership for Parks.

The result of the first 15-week segment of the project was a recognition that the anticipated vision for 21st-century urban recreation in NYC will have to emerge out of multiple attempts to frame it, and will be characterized by the following complementary dimensions and components of the vision:
- Social Practices and Cultural Narratives; An important goal of this project is to systematically document forms of social interaction and features of local and cultural value that contribute to recreational practice in form, type, process or experience, thus creating new recreational propositions that are socially, economically and environmentally sustainable. We then incorporate these features and forms into propositions that can contribute to locally driven innovation for the design of recreational space and activity.
- Processes, Protocols, Policies and Norms; We include surveys of regulations, rules and protocols devised by city agencies and affiliated groups in order to create, organize and maintain recreational opportunities in New York City. We pay particular attention to the tools and methods that primary designers, planners, policy makers and advocates employ to identify the goals and ideas within their constituencies as they plan and deploy initiatives for change. Throughout this project we will propose new tools and methods, as well as the modification of tools and methods that are currently used through the framework of sustainable social innovation.
- Infrastructures; The material infrastructure needed for urban recreation is certainly another important element that brings together many constituencies and requires a variety of domain experts to develop successfully. Here too we create visions for forms of urban recreation that will rely on alternative uses of the existing infrastructure, innovative programming and different approaches to urban recreation. Investigating how different groups contribute to the production of urban infrastructure will identify new synergies among these groups. These synergies will ultimately reveal opportunities to incorporate the digital and symbolic realms of social networking and augmented reality with the physical interactions characteristic of more conventional materialist approaches to urban recreation.
- Forms, Types and Modes of Participation; The project will also explore qualitative and human-centred approaches to understanding and mapping out the experience of citizens, individuals and groups in interacting with

organizations and agencies in charge of the city's recreation infrastructure. Of particular interest will be NYC residents who are traditionally marginalized in the processes and practices of planning.

In the long term, the project will attempt to create a holistic and interrelated framework for understanding, engaging with and acting in relation to emerging urban recreation processes, practices, phenomena, forms and conditions in the context of multiple, concurrent and interconnected micro-urban ecologies.

We defined public recreation space as a continuum that unfolds on two parallel levels: tactical and strategic. On the tactical level, we framed public recreation space as an environment designed to allow for citizen participation forms and practices which have been defined by public law and policy, as well as by the cultural, political and socio-economic milieu. On the strategic level, we defined it as a complex, dynamic system in action composed of a complex nexus of agents and agencies, a web of intricate social relationships in which they are embedded, material artefacts and immaterial stimuli. This framework was chosen because of its inherently systemic sensibility, as well as for its social and experiential emphasis (Mitrasinović 2006). We also insisted that public recreation space is a communication environment defined by ensembles of interactions between people, between people and material/immaterial artefacts, and between material/immaterial forms (Rapoport 1980, 1982). Finally, we argued that public space is a loaded, dynamic social environment that works

as a site of ongoing negotiations between the manifestations of privacy and publicity. It is through such negotiations that recreation space is indeed produced by all those who have a stake in it. This particular theoretical framing was designed to challenge traditional thinking about citizens as 'users' of public recreation space, by recognizing that people do not only react to their environment but also act through it (Kattsoff 1947, Woodworth 1958).[1]

Understood this way, public space can be seen as a critical instrument of citizens across the social spectrum as they strive to influence how their public and private lives unfold, in this case in relation to urban recreation.

Since our main interest in this course was to frame public recreation space as a product of social action and cultural negotiations (Lefebvre 1991), we looked for modes and methods of spatial production that would allow us to represent cycles of social and cultural production beyond the production of material artefacts traditionally linked to the realm of public recreation. Play presented itself as an ideal vehicle because as a social construct, or as an ensemble of social relationships in action, play manifests itself in space: through play, social relationships are spatialized, therefore turning space into both a condition and product of play (Mitrasinović & Salen 2004). This boundary is known as the *magic circle* (Huizinga 1938). Within the magic circle, special meanings accrue and cluster around objects and behaviours. In effect, a new reality is created, a shared space that owes its existence to the relationships between players. We decided

to use principles of play (rule structures, the magic circle and metagaming) both as a research and as a design lens, when observing citizen practices in public spaces and when conceptualizing play patterns as methods of production (Salen & Zimmerman 2004).

As with public space, there is no clear conceptual closure on what play is: although psychological and anthropological studies of play have over the last century resulted in a range of descriptive models that have attempted to define what play is, in this course we used a more design-centred definition of the concept, one that connects play to the complex, systemic and democratic features of public space. For the purposes of this project, we stated that play emerges through an ensemble of relationships guiding the functioning of a system, and in many ways it is an expression of the social system it simultaneously serves and produces (Salen & Zimmerman 2004). We were specifically interested in transformative play, a special case of play that occurs when the free movement of play alters the more rigid structure from which it emerges. In relation to the course methodology, we structured the course by reworking John Chris Jones's 1970 definition that the methodological stages employed in working through the project: Divergence, Transformation and Convergence (Jones 1970). For us, the stages not only framed three distinct phases but, more important, served as markers of time that enabled more precise field research and understanding across cultural, logistical and geographic domains within the NYC metropolitan region (Leonard & Rayport 1997).

COURSE DESCRIPTION

In the spring 2009 at the Urban Play and Recreation studio, students were asked to research and design selected components of the comprehensive vision for the future of urban recreation in NYC.

Urban Recreation Phenomena

A key objective was to understand how citizens engage in both recognized and alternative forms of play and recreation in public space and city parks and to understand how to distinguish the components of any (urban) game or recreational activity in order to develop sets of common attributes that create what we called 'playspace' (Steps 1 and 2). The attempt was to recognize, analyse, catalogue and create taxonomies of standard and non-standard recreational practices in NYC as a series of case studies.

Step 1: Playing and Documenting a Game
In this step students were asked to document a game of their choice. The goal was to clearly document every aspect of the game from its inception to its completion and to diagram its components and its time frame.

Step 2: People, Places and Practices
In this step students were asked to seek out, map and document the phenomenon of urban recreation in public space.

Participatory Design Methods and Tools

Another goal was to examine if and how citizens take part in participatory processes, in co-designing and in providing feedback related to urban recreation. An objective to determine the different ways organizations gather information from constituents and stakeholders and translate them into the data useful for designers of parks and other recreational sites. The aims were to develop tools for gathering and interpreting the information (Step 3) and to develop protocols that allow citizens to organize themselves independently.

Step 3: Hester Street Collaborative Participatory Design Tools
In this step our team visited the Hester Street Collaborative (HSC). During this visit HSC presented their participatory design tools and engaged the team in one of their activities: The Walking Tour. In small groups, students analysed and documented this experience.

Organizations and Actors

The objective of this component was to identify all the participants involved in the process of park design and examine the roles different organizations and actors play in this process, the kind of strategies they use to collaborate and share information among themselves and the sites of interaction (i.e. where, when and how interagency interactions occur) (Step 4). Students and faculty worked on developing tools that would facilitate more effective interactions between organizations whose mission is to design, organize, develop, maintain and manage urban parks and public space.

Step 4: Persona Development
In this step, our team studied roles of organizations and individuals that participate in designing recreational public spaces in NYC. Student teams built personas of fictitious characters as repositories of the knowledge gathered about the participating organizations and to simulate relationships between different stakeholders involved in this process. For this purpose we used the list of groups and organizations involved in the development of the East River Park and the Allen and Pike Street Malls provided by the Hester Street Collaborative.

Step 5: Scenario-Building
In the second half of the semester, students were introduced to the notion of scenario-building, understood as a tool for promoting strategic conversation among the stakeholders (van der Heiden 2005) and developing hypotheses (not predictions) and provocative stories (Scearce, Fulton & the Global Business Network community 2004) in order to portray several possible design solutions. Each student team developed a scenario to address aspects of recreation phenomena, organizations or participatory methods in order to frame specific questions, present tentative strategies and stimulate conversations with our partners. Students produced storyboards to visualize their ideas. During this process we continuously discussed students' ideas with our partners for the purpose of receiving critical feedback

and validation. The methodological objective of the course was to, at this point, identify at least one 'concept opportunity' per student.

Step 6: Concept Generation

Each of the scenarios provided a context for multiple equally plausible concepts, which gave students an opportunity to develop individual concept-propositions while remaining within the team framework. After concept opportunities were identified, students developed projects that could work in a systemic way as components of the urban recreation ecologies framework as well as individual leads that could be addressed independently and could generate a range of actionable insights for elaboration in future courses.

Propositions

The class has generated a wealth of ideas, approaches, scenarios, actionable ideas and projects. Sam Crumpton and Katherine O'Brien developed two different concepts for involving citizens in documenting recreational practices across New York City and creating a comprehensive database that could be accessed by anyone but would explicitly be used by Hester Street Collaborative to organize, catalogue and classify a wealth of images documenting urban recreation in the city (Figure 1). Individual citizens would document recreational practices of interest

Figure 1: Documenting recreational practices across New York City. Concept by Katherine O'Brien.

and upload tagged images to the Wiki-driven and Web-based interface powered by Google Earth. Images would be organized by zip codes, locations taken, season, etc. The objective was to provide urban researchers, park designers and the Parks and Recreation Department's Capital Projects division with a database that can be used to identify contemporary and future needs that are socially and geographically distributed across the five boroughs. In addition, Christina DiPaci proposed an infrastructure

for juxtaposing images of future or past use in physical locations where current uses are unsatisfactory or under revision. Such images deployed in parks and sites of urban recreation would create a dialogue and inspire citizen participation in neighbourhood groups and community organizations in order to bring desirable changes to urban recreation spaces in their neighbourhoods.

Naomi Otsu developed an ethnographic research tool designed as a game board,

(1) Hester Street Collaborative holds an event that gets people motivated about improving their recreational space. Community members sign up for the PlaySpace program.

(2) Participants from the community keep an eye out for sights that depict what they want for their local recreational spaces.

(3) They snap a picture of it and send or upload it to the PlaySpace image database under their name along with geolocational data.

40° 43' 51" N, 73° 59' 51" W

(4) The image is worked into a large mosaic map of the area along with other images according to where the participant lives.

(5) i wish my park had more trees than trash cans...

The participant can use tags and notes to provide an explanation of the image and why it has been uploaded.

(6) The result is (a) an ever-growing work of art created by the community and (b) statistical information that can be used by Hester Street to determine what the community needs in a recreational space.

intended for designers of urban play environments to be able to arrive at a deeper understanding of the areas of intervention and the drivers, motivators and triggers that enable meaningful citizen participation in the processes of design, use and interpretation. The tool is meant to develop empathic skills in designers and allow them to effectively gather ethnographic data needed for their ongoing projects (Figure 2).

In order to rethink interagency communication, Jessica Liftman developed a persona-creation kit composed of standard elements. The aim of this kit is to function as a repository of information about all the organizations involved in the conceptualization, design and maintenance of urban parks. The strength of this tool is in visualizing and memorizing the qualitative information about organizational assets that commonly gets lost in the daily practices of organizing the complex system of urban recreation ecologies – and proposing a playful way of doing so. In addition, Jessica Einhorn proposed a system, based on the basic features of game play, for reorganizing community board meetings in ways that reduce the urge towards competitive behaviour by allowing each participant to create polls and to vote in them. Community board meetings can be politically challenging environments that restrict the capacity to openly exchange information, communicate and provide feedback to one another. This tool redefines the goals in such a way that participants are encouraged to collaborate through the use of this simple game system with standardized elements and simple rules of engagement.

Figure 2: The 'Respace' ethnographic research tool box. Concept by Naomi Otsu.

COMPLIMENT   RE-CONSIDERATION   IMMEDIATE ACTION

Figure 3: The 'Heal Our Park' badges for urban annotation. Concept by Nancy N. Brown.

Because it was of particular interest to our team to create platforms that would enable Partnership for Parks to reach out to its diverse audiences and enable alternative forms of engagement and participation in local parks, some students focused on developing non-technical interfaces that could be easily implemented. Nancy Brown proposed a multi-player game to take place on 'Heal Our Parks' days, whereby individuals and groups would place large colour-coded 'band-aids' in park areas that needed improvement. This approach expands the process of participation by building trust and providing a simple way to gather information. It also fosters park stewardship and face-to-face interaction amongst members of the community around a common and positive goal (Figure 3). Meryl Vedros designed a concept for a newspaper stand that would be placed in NYC parks and contain local park stewardship groups' newsletters, information on how to get involved in maintaining local parks, and contact information for city agencies and community organizations in charge of recreational spaces and urban parks. Chantelle Fuoco designed a system that brings community-based non-profit groups dedicated to urban parks together with local schools, in order to introduce concepts of community engagement and park stewardship to children in K-5 grades. Rostislav Roznoshchik proposed a multiplayer game whose purpose is the creation of collaborative local networks to share knowledge of urban recreation situated in specific communities. Using Partnership for Parks Academy as the site and context, Rostislav's treasure hunt-based game leads community members through the discovery of the geography, ecology and socio-economic aspects of park design.

CONCLUSION

As stated in the introduction, this course has enabled us to establish a long-term, five-point research and learning framework for working with the NYC Department of Parks and Recreation towards understanding objectives of urban recreation in the 21st century. The course also clearly indicates the School's attempt to move away from one-off and short-term partnerships towards long-term, strategic partnerships based no longer on the client-designer relationships that had previously rendered the School a provider of design services, but on a common interest to learn together about complex emerging phenomena and to begin to devise strategies of addressing them adequately. The reframed relationship between city agencies and academia, based on the mutual quest to learn, has proven successful in this particular experiment and has already created interest in expanding partnerships to other city agencies. The School is currently planning to initiate similar partnerships with the NYC Department of Education, the NYC Department of Transportation, the NYC Office of Customer Relations, and others. In parallel, in spring 2010, we are continuing with the second phase of our collaboration with the Department of Parks and Recreation and in the future plan to link a variety of courses and fields across Parsons and the University by thematically exploring urban processes in New York City in innovative, integrative and transdisciplinary ways.

---

[1] In the 1950s, Robert Woodworth, Louis Kattsoff and other members of the future Environment-Behavior Studies Group attempted to understand situations (environments) in which humans make choices and mechanisms through which human choice behaviour occurs. They had based their theories on the central idea of 'value', claiming that an individual does not 'react to' his environment but 'acts through' it (Kattsoff 1947, Woodworth 1958).

AUTHOR / Ina Šuklje Erjavec

CHAPTER / Designing an urban park as a contemporary user-friendly place

INTRODUCTION

Green spaces assume a key role in efforts towards enhancing the urban environment and improving the quality of urban life: they make cities more liveable places and help sustain ideals. They affect the townscape, city and neighbourhood identity, provide ecological diversity, have relevance for healthy citizens and societal well-being, represent public values and even deliver important economic benefits (GreenKeys-Team 2008). For a long time, these issues were not recognized as important, but in recent years urban green themes have been the subject of more and more research, heightened public awareness and political attention.

Owing to their spatial and functional characteristics, urban green spaces exist in a great variety of shapes, structures and types. Social developments and changing lifestyles and values influence the functions and typology of urban green spaces, which is becoming more complex and heterogeneous.

The urban park is perhaps the most complex type among contemporary urban green spaces. It should fulfil a wide range of functions. Usually located in the city centre, it plays an important role in the city's image, so it has to be representative in character and well designed, with symbolic and unique features that make it clearly recognizable. But it should also serve as a green space for everyday use by citizens and visitors. That means responding to different needs and expectations, providing an easy access and offering choices (GreenKeys 2008, Šuklje 2001).

Several authors suggest that the role of the urban park in contemporary and future cities should be rethought and developed according to new lifestyles, values and attitudes (Tschumi 1983, Thompson 2002, Turner 2004, Loukaitou-Sideris 2006). Their opinions differ and sometimes even conflict. Many authors stress the importance of experiencing nature while visiting an urban park (Thompson 2002, Kaplan & Kaplan 1989), while others introduce completely new views on the role of urban parks by emphasizing a wide variety of programmes and cultural activities to take place in the park area (Park de la La Villette 1983), thus replacing the traditional idea of the park with the new model of the 'urban park building' (Tschumi 1983). What changes are really necessary requires additional research and discussion, but it's clear that traditional ways of using and developing an urban park are no longer sufficient. User-friendly urban parks should go beyond recreation (Turner 2004), serve new needs and provide new activities and experiences (Thompson 2002, Loukaitou-Sideris 2006).

This paper explores possible design approaches to contemporary and future urban parks through the case of the *Severni mestni park-Navje* urban park project for Ljubljana, Slovenia (Šuklje et al. 1984-2009).

KEY PRINCIPLES FOR DESIGNING A USER-FRIENDLY URBAN PARK

The challenge for the landscape architect when designing the new urban park is not only to understand the new park's location and urban meaning but also the relation between users and uses. Through the design process he/she must answer the questions such as: *How to make a programme idea spatial? How to make a space communicative? How to face the need for change over time?* Answering these questions is a very complex and demanding task that entails going beyond spatial design principles in order to follow social changes over time. At the same time firm links to the place and aspiring to sustainability have to be maintained. To be user-friendly, urban parks should not only provide spaces for recreation but also propose new uses and challenge citizens to use and take ownership of them.

In the *Severni mestni park-Navje* project, a multilevel, multifunctional and flexible design considered all the key principles for designing a user-friendly and spatially responsible urban park: responding to site characteristics by using the potentials of space and location; developing the identity of the place; conceiving a clear structure and design; and creating suitable spatial possibilities for different activities and experiences that are equally accessible to all.

The park's location is in a newer, northern part of the city centre, near the main public transport terminal. The surrounding neighbourhood is a high density residential and commercial area with schools and a theatre, but with poor quality green areas. This implies a great number and variety of park users and park-user needs.

Although quite large for Ljubljana, the park site is without any major spatial quality and not really recognizable as an integral site. It is very detached, composed of more or less abandoned buildings and areas that are used as illegal or provisional car parks. The only part with a positive identity is the old memorial cemetery *Navje*, a national cultural monument where many Slovenian cultural personalities

Figure 1: 1 Park site location.

are buried. That imbues the place with strong cultural and symbolic importance, but because it is protected as a cultural monument, the site is fenced, which makes integration into the new park quite difficult. Easier to integrate are views of Ljubljana Castle and the Alps.

From the very beginning of the design process, it was clear that the park's completion would require much time, long-term planning and flexibility. The idea was to create a striking design concept that establishes a strong identity via a recognizable main structure and 'flexible spatial frames' in which cultural and everyday park activities could be developed.

In this way the park could acquire a clearly defined meaning, identity and importance derived from its location and the national cultural monument, but also respond to a wide variety of needs and expectations over time. Cultural features and activities have been emphasized in a

way that allows the landscape's character to dominate and the visitor to experience nature. This results in positive identity.

The park's design is based on symbolic and representative meanings, broader urban demands and important future uses. Its north-south linear orientation incorporates the cemetery and views of the castle and the Alps. At the same time it establishes a crucial urban connection that was missing in this part of the city. The landscape forms the core of the park, responding to the basic needs of experiencing nature, relaxation and free recreation. It is designed as an open landscape of meadows and groups of trees that offer a peaceful retreat from urban activities and open space whose visual effect and dimension soothes the eye. The circle path links the park's different parts into a recognizable whole. It connects areas for playing, strolling and meeting while surrounding and buffering the inner, more peaceful space from the

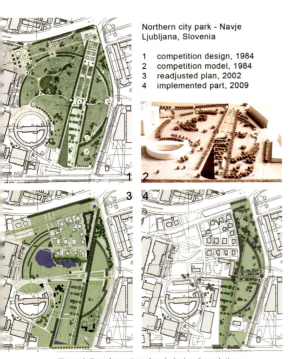

Northern city park - Navje
Ljubljana, Slovenia

1   competition design, 1984
2   competition model, 1984
3   readjusted plan, 2002
4   implemented part, 2009

Figure 2: Transformation of park design through time.

park's more active edges, where myriad activities can cater to a range of interests.

The period between the first official project (1988) and the beginning of its implementation (2004) was much longer than expected. During these 15 years new proposals and ideas were developed and places and elements in the park designed. The original park design was partly 'modernized' and adapted to new spatial

development demands. In 2003, the Civil Society Initiative called *"Društvo Rastoča knjiga"*, which can be literally translated as "Growing Book Association", asked the city of Ljubljana to find a location for a monument promoting a reading culture. Thus a new inspiration for the design of the park was given and an area of the park was redesigned for this purpose. Later on the initiative grew into the idea to represent the world's most important books throughout the park in a step by step way, that enhanced the park's symbolic and cultural meaning. How to present them, how many countries will join the action and when remain open questions, but the park's overall appearance and function must not be disturbed. The concept will be linked, however, to the other cultural and representative parts of the park.

The cultural aspects of the park became much emphasized, but the final redesign included many other elements and thematic places that are interesting for a wide variety of uses. The idea of grounds for different activities was developed further, especially in places for youngsters and children. For equipped areas a more playful design was used to attract children and youngsters and

coloured light   hidden loud-speakers and lights

bench   touch-screen display   titles of presented books

Figure 4: Places for youngsters and children.

express the vibrancy. Special multifunctional elements of wooden and rubber waves and spheres serve different uses and activities and are attractive as meeting and orientation points. Youngsters can enjoy their own space, challenge their imagination and develop a positive attitude towards the park as a whole.

To make the park user-friendly, special attention has been paid to vulnerable groups of people. All the entrances to the park, the main paths and even part of the main playground with a special roundabout are adapted for the disabled. For older visitors, comfortable benches are provided along all paths. Children's playgrounds include both sunny and shady areas.

Figure 3: Multimedia book portals.

Figure 5: 'Planned flexibility'.

Along the existing graveyard *Navje*, the so called 'Slovenian culture promenade" has been designed as a representative linear motive connecting the park with a wider urban area, incorporating views to the caste and Alps, as well as the 'motives of books' within the newly arranged 'Square of literature'. The design of the whole area incorporates the themes of culture and literature into the physical fabrics (e.g. the iron pavement plates that can be cut out into sentences, an asphalt path and concrete murals that can be painted by children, a temporary open space gallery on an old building façade, a fountain with a monument) and allows flexibility over time.

CONCLUSION

Discussion and practical experience indicate that user-friendly urban parks should embody sound structure and landscape design, express a clear identity, and be adaptable to changing needs, attitudes and values.

Because of its spatial and typological characteristics as well as planning, design and implementation processes going on for along time, the above presented park of *Severni mestni park-Navje* is a valuable example of the urban park design that is maintaining the identity of place in spite of changes to the overall project. Its original concept has been developed over time to meet new demands but its main structure with all its basic elements of spatial identity have remained the same. Although its linear south-north motive has been spatially reduced (narrowed) and redesigned into the 'Slovenian cultural promenade', the park has maintained its representative character. A later on added element of the design concept – 'the growing books' – supported the original idea of the park's cultural programmes and activities and became one of its key elements. Similarly the circle path will remain a key element of the park due to its recognizable form and emphasised by trees, lights and relief, although it will probably not be completed as originally conceived. Also the inside of the park that facilitates recreation activities reminds open and flat as initially planned but the edges of the park have been designed afresh into a hilly landscape to form a safe and clearly defined park space, with playing activities incorporated. Although some more significant changes have been made at a detailed level to better meet the current and possibly future needs and tastes, the overall appearance of the park stays firm and well recognizable.

AUTHOR / Barbara Goličnik Marušić

CHAPTER / Designing public places with users in mind

INTRODUCTION

Urban design with users in mind is crucial to public open spaces in city centres, such as squares and parks, and to the activities carried out within them. Therefore, the characteristics of the events they might host, the public's needs and expectations, and opportunities for a variety of uses – from passive to active, from spontaneous to organized – designers should bear on their design. This chapter, written with a designer's curiosity and rigour, addresses these issues using data collected from observation and behaviour-mapping in two European cities, Edinburgh, UK (May 2002) and Ljubljana, Slovenia (May 2003; June 2006).

Owing to a variety of reasons, such as the flow of capital and commercial and residential development pressure, urban planning and design is currently a very dynamic field. In such a context open spaces are constantly exposed to two main, often conflicted interests. They are often cultural landmarks that bring added value and a higher quality of life to residents, yet they are jeopardized by rapid development and prioritizing private over public interests. Especially on a small scale, overbearing private interests can result in programmatic impoverishment and mono-functionality, e.g. crowding of squares and pedestrian areas with outdoor bars, cafés and restaurants, while neglecting other socially conducive programmes.

This chapter addresses the use of places. Public open space is understood as a publicly or privately owned, publicly accessible environment defined by a continuous relationship between its physical structure and sets of (possible) events.

SUCCESSFUL PUBLIC OPEN SPACE

Addressing successful public spaces in cities, Gehl & Gemzøe argue two crucial points: *vandare necesse est*, 'walking is essential', and 'once we take the subject of creating good and worthy surroundings for foot traffic seriously, the next step is to ensure that people can sit down to rest and relax along the way. Benches and café chairs enter the picture. A section of booths and shops also becomes relevant so that pedestrians can look and shop while they walk. The social aspect comes into play' (Gehl & Gemzøe 2001: 257).

This understanding, while thoughtful and essential, expresses quite general view of design and exemplifies the types of engagement that will attract most adults. In public place design, there is a need for more precise understanding of spatiality, place usage, and user-groups and their interaction with places. Such comprehensive and inclusive way could better integrate the social aspect and enhance the general perspective. It can inform the design of (potential) places, which may encourage longer engagements and provide formal (cafés, benches) and informal settings for passive contemplation, enjoying a coffee or window shopping – in short, a public space that welcomes everyone.

In comparison with public spaces in general, public open spaces offer a greater variety of uses. For example, loose-fit places or their parts can be even more appropriate and attractive to the development of spontaneous and informal uses. The presence of people is key to successful public places (PPS 2005; Cooper Marcus & Francis 1998; Gehl 1987). Cooper

Marcus & Francis (1998), for example, stress the importance of location, user presence and a diversity of activities, programmes, equipment and comfort (possibilities of shade, shelter from wind, etc.). Meanwhile, a diversity of choice either in terms of programme (What can people do in places? What is it possible to do in the buildings surrounding an open space?, etc.), urban furniture or physical layout influences the variety of uses in places.

Environmental possibilism and environmental probabilism, notions from the field of environmental psychology, have been known for decades. However, design practice still very much reflects environmental determinism, or the notion that circumstances have an absolute causal relationship to events: the environment determines use and a place itself is an important spatial result that users are invited to accept and become familiar with. When a certain public place actually offers choices and/ or stimulates different types of uses, such a place goes beyond environmental determinism and follows the principles of environmental possibilism and/or probabilism. Environmental possibilism is seen as 'the notion that the environmental context makes possible some activities but does not force them to occur' (Bell et al. 2001: 511). In other words, people can choose from the range of environmental opportunities offered by a certain physical setting. Environmental probabilism is defined as 'the notion that the environmental context makes some activities more probable than the others but does not absolutely determine which will occur' (Bell et al. 2001: 511). However, public space is a two-way process:

people produce and modify spaces, while spaces influence people in various ways.

SEARCH FOR EMPIRICAL KNOWLEDGE OF USAGE-SPATIAL RELATIONSHIP

Evaluation of design proposals with regard to usage-spatial relationships can increase the chance of place design success, and enhance understanding of place capacity for certain types of occupancy. Such knowledge can help designers deal with the flexibility of places, e.g. recognize a place's capacity to transform and respond to change, and might help designers avoid situations to which Lynch alludes: 'Most often, when a designer says to himself that he is being flexible, in reality he is only being vague. By failing to define structure or allocation, he is simply shifting the responsibility for decision to other individuals, or to the play of circumstance. Chaos or lack of structure is not flexible per se' (Lynch in Banerjee & Southworth 1991: 252).

Behaviour maps: tools for gathering information about place usage

Generally, behaviour maps enable the examination of real usage-spatial relationships on a 1:1 scale. Behaviour data collection requires thorough preparation. Before recording, it is necessary to obtain an accurate scale map of the area to be observed, to define the entire observation period, to schedule specific times and their repetitions for observation, to choose

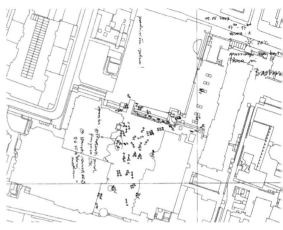

Figure 1: Example of behaviour map produced in the field, Trg republike, Ljubljana.

the types and details of behaviours to be observed, and to finalize a list of anticipated activities, their related symbols and additional coding (age groups, activity duration, etc.). It is important during the observation to stay open-ended for any possible new activity, and to be prepared for the definition of attached symbols for unexpected or infrequent activities.

Behaviour maps provide a shorthand description of the distribution of behaviours throughout the place. The major value of behaviour maps, as a research tool, lies in the possibility of developing general principles regarding the use of space that apply in a variety of settings. When one combines behaviour-mapping and GIS techniques to reveal common patterns of behaviour that

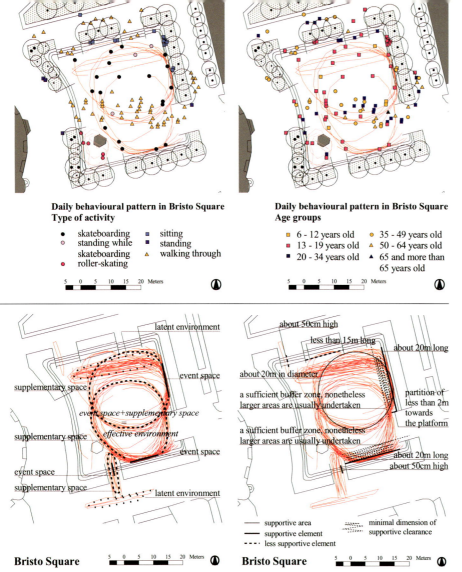

Daily behavioural pattern in Bristo Square
Type of activity

- ● skateboarding
- ◍ standing while skateboarding
- ● roller-skating
- ■ sitting
- ■ standing
- ▲ walking through

5 0 5 10 15 20 Meters

Daily behavioural pattern in Bristo Square
Age groups

- ▫ 6 - 12 years old
- ▪ 13 - 19 years old
- ■ 20 - 34 years old
- ○ 35 - 49 years old
- △ 50 - 64 years old
- ▲ 65 and more than 65 years old

5 0 5 10 15 20 Meters

latent environment
event space
supplementary space
event space+supplementary space
effective environment
supplementary space
event space
supplementary space
latent environment

Bristo Square   5 0 5 10 15 20 Meters

about 50cm high
less than 15m long
about 20m long
about 20m in diameter
a sufficient buffer zone, nonetheless larger areas are usually undertaken
partition of less than 2m towards the platform
a sufficient buffer zone, nonetheless larger areas are usually undertaken
about 20m long
about 50cm high

— supportive area
━ supportive element
┅ less supportive element
⋯ minimal dimension of supportive clearance

Bristo Square   5 0 5 10 15 20 Meters

appear to be correlated with particular layouts and details, the resulting GIS behaviour maps compile behaviour evidence into layers of spatial information that provide a better understanding of the individual and collective patterns of use that emerge in a place. The overlap of behaviour maps can show some characteristics and changes in using chosen open spaces in terms of activities, number of people engaged, gender, and all the other variables that are explored. To show the role and value of GIS behaviour maps in design practice, Goličnik (2007: 136) stresses, 'GIS behaviour map concentrates on the relationship between the spatial characteristics of place and the dynamic of its use, which is a field where the empirical basis for the design decision-making process is lacking and new techniques offering more reliable ways of predicting and understanding use are therefore valuable tools'. For some examples of GIS behaviour maps referring to different types of information which can be generated and interpreted from the behaviour map, see figures 2 and 3.

Figure 2: Typical example of daily occupancy in Bristo Square, Edinburgh, arranged with regard to the type of activity and age group to which a participant belongs.

Figure 3: Inner structure of skateboarders' behaviour patterns revealed as the event, supplementary, effective and latent environments for skateboarders in Bristo Square, Edinburgh; and dimensions of supportive and disruptive environments for skateboarders, compiled from the cumulative evidence represented on assembly behaviour maps of Bristo Square, Edinburgh.

Figure 4: Skateboarding at Bristo Square, Edinburgh.

This square was not planned as a skateboarders' platform but a certain spatial articulation has stimulated its users to be there and to use it for their pastime. However, this certain articulation in itself does not ensure optimal use. The size, shape and vertical articulation of the available space are of key importance, see figures 3 and 4.

Behaviour maps: scripts of empirical knowledge of public space use

GIS is an effective practical tool to build, develop and maintain a body of empirical knowledge using GIS interactive behaviour maps as its scripts. Organized GIS layers in such scripts make it easy to arrange a selection of relevant usage-spatial relationship variables, which function as a convenient tool for monitoring and updating designers' tacit knowledge of changes and trends in place use. Such databases can assemble empirical knowledge about stimulating and inhibitive environments for single or multiple occupancies. Concerning the implementation of such knowledge in open public space design, operationally, visualization of research findings and its related concerns to decision-making, evaluation and management is of key importance. The practical value of this tool is in how it helps designers be confident that the layouts proposed for intended uses will, in practice, serve those uses (and users) well and be likely to be used as predicted.

Figure 5: Conducive environments for sitting in a park.

Tivoli   5 0 5 10 15 M

Princes Street Gardens   5 0 5 10 15 M

Tivoli   5 0 5 10 15 M

the Meadows   5 0 5 10 15 M

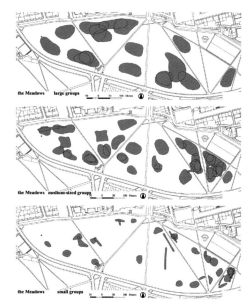

Figure 6: Large, medium and small groups involved in any active long-stay activity on all the days within the whole observation period in the Meadows, Edinburgh (Long-stay activity is any activity that was carried out for more than five minutes within a single ten-minute observation period).

Goličnik (2005) finds that when a physical edge is present in a place such as park or square, e.g. a wall or slope, people typically sit right next to it. When the edge is semi-transparent, such as a row of trees along a park path, people usually sit at least five metres away from the boundary. The width of the buffer area depends on the size, shape and articulation of the main green patch defined by such semi-transparent edges.

On park green patches of about 25,000 m², the buffer zone between a tree-lined path and the sitting area can reach up to 15 metres (see Figure 5). Some general research (Gehl 1987; Whyte 1980; Project for Public Space 2005) and observation (Goličnik 2005) reveal that when comfortable microclimatic conditions occur in spatially defined, recognized niches, back-covered and having a nice view are the crucial aspects of choosing where to sit down in a public place.

Not only spatial articulation, per se, but also the articulation that is achieved by dimensions uses create in public spaces, especially groups, can provide available areas within places for usage, articulate available spaces and by this create places. Size and shape of green patches are not particularly crucial to passive use as long as they are big enough to exceed 5m width from transparent edges. According to Goličnik & Ward Thompson (2010), empirical data also show that the minimum distance between individuals and groups who sit down in the grass is four metres, which provides comfort and a sense of privacy in a public space. An edge is important for passive use; for active use, such as playing or sports, the space's openness, shape and size are more important. An informal game of football (15-20 persons) requires a longitudinally shaped area of 3,000 to 5,000 m². For smaller groups, less than 3,000 m² is sufficient. Space for frisbee-throwing can be quite narrow but requires length, while various ball games require a space whose length does not exceed double its width (see Figure 6).

CONCLUSION

To achieve responsive environments and good urban design practice, it is important to consider that designers and planners create potential environments, places of opportunities and possibilities, while people create effective environments, places of actual uses and realized opportunities. Therefore, regarding design decision-making and public space management, it is important to know and understand usage-spatial relationships. Based on empirical knowledge about usage-spatial relationships, it is possible to stimulate admissible and/or compatible uses.

GIS behaviour maps are recognized as an effective tool to represent and interpret behaviour patterns as visual data. They also translate recorded evidence into a body of empirical knowledge and preserve the connection of related non-spatial data (age, gender, activity type, etc.) to the material place. Mapping physical dimensions of uses is thus seen as a potential way of negotiating forms of places.

AUTHOR / Matej Nikšič

CHAPTER / Mapping a perceptual dimension of open urban public space

INTRODUCTION

The importance of the representation of the open urban space in the mental image of users and its influence on the usage of space has been acknowledged in urban design and related disciplines for decades (Bachelard 1957; Rasmussen 1964; Downs & Stea 1973; Tuan 1977; Lynch 1981). It is commonly agreed that the mental conceptions greatly influence decisions on usage of space. Thus it is important to understand mental representations of space in the minds of its users in order to design spaces that will actually be used.

Promising current research in the fields of neuroscience, environmental psychology, and context-aware computing, and common endeavours in interdisciplinary research, has led to new discoveries in the field of spatial perception. They are applied to new, pioneering disciplines (electronic devices and ambient intelligence, for example) that assume people make decisions based on their mental perceptions of the world they live in, and that the effect they anticipate their actions will have on their own inner world influences these actions.

Nevertheless, the incorporation of this new and rapidly developing knowledge is applied in spatial planning practice only with hesitation. Although new approaches have been developed that incorporate perceptual dimensions of space into the design process (Thwaites & Simkins 2007; Nold not dated) and some of aspects of spatial perception have been studied in detail (Pallasmaa, 2005, Barbara & Perliss 2006), the cognitive dimensions of space are often neglected by mainstream urban planning.

USER PERCEPTION AND APPRECIATION OF THE URBAN ENVIRONMENT

Discourses on environmental psychology and the philosophy of aesthetics have revealed that the perception and appreciation of a given environment is a complex phenomenon that depends on a number of factors arising from every individual observer (Bell et al. 2001; von Bonsdorff 2002; Macauley 2007). Given this conditionality, creating an environment that will be appreciated by everyone is impossible. What some people like, others dislike and vice

versa (Rasmussen 1959; Merleau-Ponty 2005). However, this fact must not obstruct future endeavours in this field; on the contrary– new tools and approaches need to be developed.

While the pioneering approaches that incorporated perceptual dimensions into urban design were focused mainly on visual and kinesthetic aspects of spatial perception (Lynch 1960; Cullen 1961; Appleyard 1980), a shift towards behavioural aspects occurred at the turn of the 21st century (Passini 1992; Ward Thompson et al. 2005; Goličnik 2005; Thwaites & Simkins 2007). Some of the new methods and techniques are based on analyses by experts who act as skilled observers, while others are based more on the fact that the mental image of a given space depends on the individual, thus more direct and participatory methods are necessary. Fortunately, such methods are more easily achieved than ever before, as new technical devices enable individuals to directly communicate their perceptions of the world they live in.

In the following paragraphs such a method is outlined. This method aims to reveal the perception and appreciation of open urban spaces by users directly involved in the studied space. It is an attempt to reveal individual notions of space, specifically, of what constitutes open urban space in the minds of its users, not only in terms of overall content but also in terms of (un) appreciation of certain elements.

A COMBINED INTERVIEWING AND SKETCHING TECHNIQUE

As the mental representation of the environment is not a selective abstraction of reality but rather an *interpretation* of what is and what is not *believed* to be (Relph 1976), insight cannot be gained unless the user of the space is directly involved in collecting data. According to Kvale (1996), the most appropriate way of getting to know someone's notions is by interview him/her. The interview enables the interviewer to listen to what people have to say about the world they live in, and hear their points of view and opinions in their very own words. It appears to be a very suitable technique for revealing the mental images of individuals. Choosing an interview as a research technique represents a shift away from conventional practice, where the user remained an object of scholarly observation and investigation rather than an active player in the process of investigation.

In order to localize the issues exposed by the interviewees, the interview as a research technique is complemented by a sketch on a morphological map of the studied space. Thus a twofold device (Nikšič 2008) – a combination of oral examination and sketching– is established with the following aims:

– oral examination is used to uncover users' personal appreciations and beliefs related to the studied space, such as what, in their opinion, characterizes that space and which of the identified characteristics are liked or disliked by users;

– sketching on the morphological map is used to reveal the extensions of studied space in users' mental images in relation to the physical space. By applying this technique the examiner receives detailed insight into which components of the physical space are being perceived by a user's mental image as part of a studied area and which are not.

All data is ideally stored and processed electronically in the form of GIS maps and attached attribute tables. This also allows an immediate comparison with any other data related to the studied space and helps designers to better understand the space. This technique is called INSEM (INterviewing-Sketching-EMapping).

The information gained by INSEM is broad because the interviewee is free to raise any subject that seems relevant to him/her. Therefore, the examiner faces a challenging task when analysing and interpreting data. Nevertheless, the effort is well worth the gain of in-depth insight into the perceptual dimensions of space. This is of much help to those who have to redesign, improve, upgrade, modify or conceptualize a concrete open public space. The following inputs to the design process can be obtained by using INSEM:

1. What really belongs to the studied space according to the mental perceptions of its users and why this is so.
2. Which components of the studied physical space are not perceived as part of it in users' mental images and why this is so.
3. The objective characteristics of space (physical, programmatic or symbolic in nature) that constitute its image in users' minds and denotes which of these characteristics are appreciated (i.e. have a positive connotation) or not appreciated (i.e. have a negative connotation) in users' opinions.

Through a representative sampling and an appropriate number of interviews, a common perceptual image of the studied place can be compiled. The designer of space is thus given an extra and otherwise invisible layer of information, which in addition to other spatial information (such as morphology studies, analyses of programmes, uses and movement and behavioural patterns, etc.)

Figure 1: An interviewee at sketching.

forms a comprehensive and multilayered set of information on space. Incorporating this information, decisions on concrete interventions can be much more grounded.

The practical use of the tool is demonstrated via a case study of Kongresni trg Square in Ljubljana, Slovenia (Nikšič 2008; Goličnik & Nikšič 2009). Kongresni trg Square is one of the centrally located open public spaces in the city centre of Ljubljana and was to undergo a redesign process owing to the construction of an underground garage. It is surrounded by 19th century two- and three-storey buildings and has a regular orthogonal ground plan with the exception of the southern edge, which is not parallel a straight row of buildings but rather set some distant in front of them, thus creating an extra open space. The northern part of the square is planted with mature trees while the southern part is paved and maintained as an extensive parking lot.

Technically, only the platform above the underground construction needed to be redesigned after its completion. But a more sound approach would take into account a number of other factors. One of them – a perceptual image of this space – was studied using INSEM. The results provided clear evidence that the surface above the garage was not an appropriately defined intervention area in terms of users' perceived limits of the square. The interviewed users named the perceived borders of the square elsewhere

Figure 3: Borders of Kongresni trg Square and its neighbouring spaces as perceived by four interviewees.

Figure 2: Kongresni trg Square as seen from the Ljubljana Castle on an early Sunday morning.

but following the lines of the proposed underground construction. This would remind a responsible decision-maker that the area of an intervention shall not be defined only by the technical demands of the underground garage, but rather in accordance with the existing perceived dimensions of the space in users' mental images. In other words, a

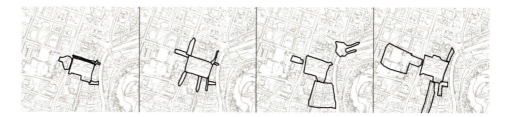

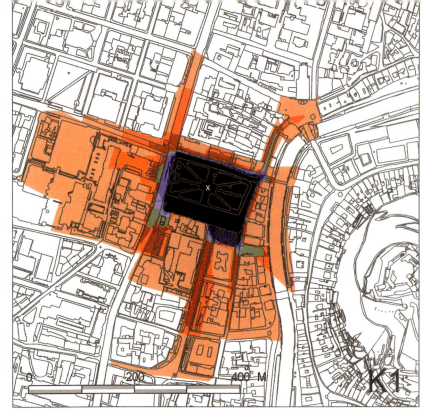

Figure 4: A common image of the perceived borders of Kongresni trg Square: the darker the blue colour is, the more the area is perceived as a constituent part of Kongresni trg Square in the mental image of its users.

wider area shall be treated in the redesign process with the same care in order to enhance the perceived wholeness of the square.

Other empty open spaces bound to the square in physical terms are not perceived as a constituent part of the square by users. What could be done to integrate them? INSEM can be helpful here, as it can reveal the most frequent reasons for the physically attached neighbouring places not to be perceived as part of the square. These were, for example, a lack of appropriate activities, the presence of few people, vehicle traffic along the perceived border, a physical barrier in the form of parked cars, etc. By knowing this, a designer is given a hint about what can be done to incorporate these spaces so they become a constituent part of the square in the mental image of its users and thus likely be used more regularly. Similarly, existing elements that users perceive as positive can be stressed and upgraded in the redesign process to further increase user appreciation.

CONCLUSION

As a mental image greatly depends on the perceptual stimuli gained from the outer world, part of revealing the mental image is asking the user to define perceived characteristics of space and to value them. The data gained by asking these questions provides in-depth insight into characteristics of space that are appreciated by users and might be upgraded or at least left untouched in the process of (re)designing open public spaces. Such information is a valuable input in the working process of experts who are in charge of conception, design and maintenance of open urban public spaces, such as urban designers, landscape architects, architects, street furniture designers, sociologists, etc. By being provided this information, along with other relevant data (such as morphological elements, programmatic schemes, movement patterns, behavioural patterns, visual qualities, etc.), they can understand the space in a much more comprehensive way and act accordingly.

AUTHORS / Biba Tominc, Nina Goršič and Breda Mihelič

CHAPTER / **Regeneration of historic sites in the city centre of Ljubljana: the role of public participation in public space design**

INTRODUCTION

The regeneration of historic sites involves both preventing their decay and preserving their historical characteristics. Interventions include measures to improve the physical, economic, social and ecological conditions of a particular area.

This chapter focuses on the methodology for planning and implementing comprehensive regeneration of city centres. In particular, it addresses historic sites that call for a more thorough and sensitive approach.

The following methodology was presented within the European research project ReUrban Mobil (ReUrban Mobil, www.re-urban.com) and implemented in Ljubljana's Miklošič Park. The methodology itself includes steps from the initial analysis based on GIS and questionnaires, through the identification of problems and potentials at the selected site,

to the presentation of various solutions for the most pressing problems. The tool to identify such problems was a participatory workshop involving local residents and authorities. To address the relationship between society and place, this chapter focuses on the role such participatory workshops have in the process of regenerating a selected area.

Miklošič Park is located in the city centre of Ljubljana. It is known for its unique Art Nouveau architectural heritage, typical 19th century urban layout and small park. Despite these important historical aspects, it faces economic, physical and social decay. The entire area is 56,280 m², which is ample for the comprehensive regeneration approach.

Specifically, it consists of six urban blocks mainly of residential use and a park (4,800 m²).

The blocks are relatively small (from 5,000 to 25,000 m²). The buildings stand along the streets in serried ranks. Their courtyards are separated by high fences, most of them are accessible via thoroughfares only on foot, though some of them allow vehicle entry. Together these back yards form a large open space within each block; they are not exploited by residents or businesses despite possessing great potential. Mihelič et al. (2005b) show that such blocks are the most suitable spatial entities for comprehensive regeneration processes on a detailed level. The research group of ReUrban Mobil showed that

Figure 1: From left to right: Maks Fabiani's design proposal for the square in front of the Palace of Justice (Der Architect, 1900, VI, p. 29); Miklošič park at the beginning of the 20th century arranged by Czech gardener Vaclav Hejnic (Historical Archives of Ljubljana); Miklošič park today.

this is also the case in other European cities, such as Bologna, Leipzig and Leon, where much urban regeneration has taken place.

In the early 20th century, Maks Fabiani designed the park as a square in front of the courthouse. Originally, it was conceived as a paved platform, but it was later transformed into a park with symmetrical tree-lines perpendicularly oriented towards the main façade of the Palace of Justice and with a circular promenade in the central part. To achieve a harmonized spatial effect all the other surrounding buildings were of the same height and with corner towers as architectural accents. Cut trees allowed open views to the surrounding architecture. After the WWII the original image of the park changed radically; the circular promenade was replaced with two diagonal paths and the trees that were allowed to grow obstruct the view of the surrounding facades (Figure 1).

COMPREHENSIVE REGENERATION METHODOLOGIES

The ReUrban Mobil project involved four partner cities, Bologna, Leipzig, Leon and Ljubljana, which examined the problems and potentials of inner city residential neighbourhoods. The objective was to develop new methods for stimulating reurbanization in such areas. The project defined reurbanization as the 'process of optimizing economic, legal, social, built and environmental conditions to provide vibrant living space within the urban core (encompassing identity and cultural heritage) where individuals and

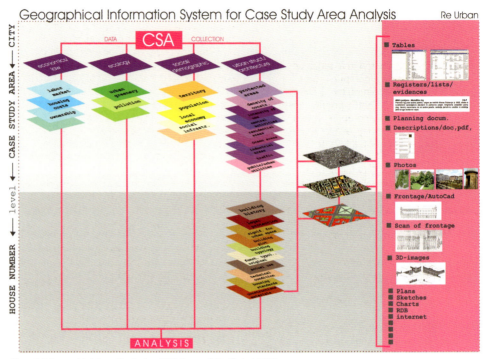

Figure 2: A Geographic Information System (GIS) diagram (Mihelič et al. 2005).

households choose to live and which attracts investment' (ReUrban Mobil).

Based on previous experiences and knowledge transfer, partners set up a comprehensive regeneration method consisting of the following steps:
- analysis based on GIS, questionnaires and participatory workshops;

- identification of area problems and potentials;
- designing a tool box (a catalogue of instruments) to encourage reurbanization.

GIS analysis was based on data collected from statistical sources (Figure 2). It addresses four main fields, which appear to be crucial to city development:
- sociology and demography;

- architecture and urban planning and design;
- economy and law;
- urban ecology.

Information was collected in a database that helped to create a computer model for analysing and evaluating the areas of regeneration, and to identify priority tasks. It acts as an objective and open system that can be applied at any level of a city, from the broader municipal level to the detailed level of an urban block. Such a system offers a possibility for an up-to-date monitoring and evaluation of existing conditions, enables a quicker response to negative trends, and encourages simultaneous adaptation of instruments and policies in order to improve the present situation.

Questionnaires and interviews were used to collect subjective data about the area and about residents' and other participants' needs, habits and wishes.

To sum up, precise analysis based on GIS and questionnaires can help to accumulate valuable knowledge about an area and is a good starting point for the evaluation of reurbanization possibilities and probabilities.

Methodology implementation in the case of Miklošič Park area

The methodology, based on GIS, questionnaires and participatory workshops, was applied in the case study area. The analysis identified problems related to

traffic, decrease of basic supply and urban facilities, poor building maintenance (structures, facades, etc.) and poor housing conditions (no lifts, lack of parking places, decaying apartments). Social and demographic problems were also identified: an aging (aging index: 200, Census 2002) and rapidly shrinking population. The latter is detrimental to the area's residential function, i.e. residential and commercial vacancy. An aging and shrinking population negatively affects the area's social status and economic potential, which consequently affects infrastructure and quality of life. Concerning ecological issues, the biggest problems are noise and air pollution, both caused by traffic. However, the rich architectural heritage, the green open space of the public park in the city centre, and many residential flats represent a great potential for the area: comprehensive reurbanization could transform it into one of the city's most liveable places.

Role of the participatory workshop in the process of comprehensive regeneration

Various international approaches to regeneration show that participatory workshops with local residents are a crucial tool for stimulating the regeneration processes. Residents have a chance to discuss, become familiar and get involved with the aims and the entire process of regeneration. Workshops usually focus on the most urgent problems and

Figure 3: Images from workshop sessions (photographs: Biba Tominc, UPIRS, 2005).

help local communities to stay in touch with regeneration planning and implementation. Communication between planners and residents is also very important. Workshops allow communication and constant feedback, which is very important in any dialogue

between local communities, authorities and planners. Effective communication between civil society, private sector and local government is one of the key factors for the sustainable urban development. In this particular case, the workshop, entitled Living and working in the city centre of Ljubljana – Miklošič Park was co-organized and co-moderated by the Urban Planning Institute of the Republic of Slovenia and the Municipality of Ljubljana. Local residents and owners of businesses and offices were invited by post to participate in the workshop.

Research analysis determined the workshop's topics of discussion:
- park renovation and improvement;
- reorganization of the courtyards;
- parking problems;
- arrangement of sheltered housing.

The workshop itself was divided into two parts. In the first part, analysis of existing conditions was presented to participants and the proposals for the improvements were explained. The second part of the workshop established four working groups. Each group discussed one of the four topics, used sketches and consulted maps (Figure 3). They identified problems and discussed the proposed solutions. Results were summed up in the final session by a representative of each group.

WORKSHOP RESULTS

The workshop results clarified:
- participants' attitudes towards the area,

regeneration and their participation in regeneration;
- problems, wishes, expectations of participants;
- common interest in regenerating the area and agreement on how it can be done.

Regeneration issues in Miklošič Park

Miklošič Park is one of the most important public open spaces in the city centre of Ljubljana. Inadequate urban furniture, tree-

Figure 4: Three options for the regeneration of the park discussed among the inhabitants and presented by an illustrator (Damjan Stepančič, on the photo above): from left to right: Fabiani's proposal; proposal by Andjelić; proposal by Vozlič.

obstructed secessionist facades and a feeling that the park serves no purpose other than spatial transition are grounds for regeneration. Some ideas for the historical development of the park and guidelines for its future management were introduced at the workshop. Workshop results showed that residents perceive the park mainly as a physical form, visually (a window view) and as a quality ecological entity (tall healthy trees). They do not recognize it as a place that could become an animated urban space with interesting facilities and amenities. Despite the problems (lack

of maintenance and urban furniture, lack of purpose, homeless people, etc.), residents feel strongly attached to the park and are happy to participate in the regeneration process. The main issues concerning the park regeneration was the dilemma related to the conservation: either restoring the park's original image subordinated to the façade of the Palace of Justice (which would mean sacrificing the existing greenery) or designing a new layout for the park (Figure 4). The participants were most in favour of a combination of the original design with new elements.

Figure 5: Some views into the courtyards (photographs: Nina Goršič and Damjana Zaviršek Hudnik, UPIRS, 2005).

Rearrangement of courtyards

The area's greatest potential are the courtyards. They represent one-third of the entire surface of the area. Detailed analysis of the courtyards of all five blocks was introduced at the workshop. Currently, back yards of the buildings are used mostly for informal parking. Some contain vegetation of no particular use (Figure 5). The examples of good practices from abroad make the residents aware how the courtyards could be developed and maintained in order to achieve better quality of place and living conditions.

The main reasons for the courtyards to be neglected are the dispersed ownerships

Figure 6: Courtyards used for parking (photographs: Nina Goršič and Damjana Zaviršek Hudnik, UPIRS, 2005).

of residential buildings and individual back yards, high border walls, and parking. The participants had very different opinions about the appropriate maintenance of the courtyards. They find the idea of common arrangement of

the courtyards interesting, but they expressed concerns about ownership and maintenance issues. Those who park cars in their back yards were absolutely against a common courtyard arrangement because, they argued, no other parking possibilities exist other than expensive parking garages. However, participants agreed that a common approach to courtyards could be possible with help of additional professional guidance and discussion.

Parking

Area parking capacity does not meet the needs of residents or the city. The entire area was analysed in detail and the possibilities to increase parking capacity for residents and employees was proposed for three of five block (Figure 6).

Workshop participants highlighted many parking problems (such as the lack of nearby

parking places, traffic noise and pollution, poor organization, etc.). They also highlighted the lack of interest shown by the Municipality of Ljubljana in solving their problems. Most residents feel that the best solution for their parking problems is to transform the courtyards into parking lots. Participants also emphasized the problem of vehicle accessibility to courtyards when intervention or renovation is needed. However, they are aware that the solution to parking problems is a process that depends on many actors and that time and patience are necessary. Residents expect close collaboration with the municipality to find a suitable solution.

Figure 7: The existing ground plan of the building and the proposal for the new sheltered housing units (Mihelič et al. 2005).

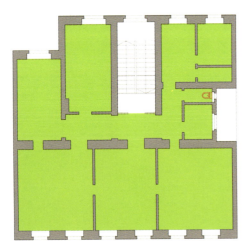

Sheltered housing in the case study area

Working group four discussed the possibility of converting an early 20th century urban residential building into sheltered apartments. The proposal entails the transformation of four flats into nine smaller units adjusted to the standards of sheltered housing and the needs of the elderly. An external elevator is added and two smaller loft flats are arranged

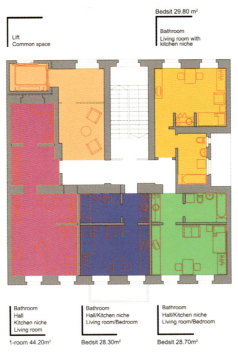

for the needs of the staff (Figure 7). Rearrangement would encourage many elderly residents to move from their larger flats into smaller units, especially as it gives them a chance to stay within an area they are familiar with. Such a measure would also solve the problems of empty or half-empty flats and their refurbishment. Residents encouraged the municipality to act on these workshop proposals as soon as possible.

CONCLUSION

The methodology that comprises a comprehensive approach to the regeneration of inner city urban areas – including buildings and open spaces – represents a step forward from the so called point-regeneration approach of a single object. It requires new financial and organizational mechanisms (Mihelič et al. 2005b) and new tools to stimulate regeneration. One of the most important tools is certainly the participation of residents and other stake holders in urban planning. The Miklošič Park workshop clearly proved that the residents are willing to cooperate in the process of regeneration, not only in the renewal of their housing but also in the regeneration of public open spaces and that they want to take part in decision-making. Although the participative approach in urban planning is not yet established in Slovenia and participants do not entirely believe that their opinions matter in final decisions, the above described experience shows that resident and local actor inclusion in the regeneration process is crucial to its success.

AUTHORS / Marko Peterlin and Aidan Cerar

CHAPTER / Supporting local participation: lessons from the PoLok project

INTRODUCTION: PUBLIC SPACE AND PUBLIC PARTICIPATION

This chapter deals with a simple question: what is the role of the local residents in the planning and designing of public space? Public space serves many different functions, but it is primarily designed to enhance the quality of life of local residents and other city users. Local residents have the deepest knowledge of their immediate neighbourhood, its use and misuse. They also know best their own needs, preferences and expectations with regard to public space in their neighbourhood, being its most frequent users. These are only two of the key reasons why the local residents should be involved in the planning and design of public space.

But this is easier said than done. There are various obstacles to successful participation. Sometimes the general public and local residents do not have the adequate knowledge or experience to participate, or they simply do not wish to participate because they cannot envision individual or collective benefit. Even more often, institutions responsible for planning, planners or urban designers are not properly qualified to include local residents in the design processes constructively.

It would be unrealistic to expect a spontaneous evolution of public participation. National and local institutions have to foster participation systematically, otherwise, participation in spatial planning can be reduced to nimbyism (NIMBY: Not In My Back Yard). In order to improve it, participation has to be analysed thoroughly as a social phenomenon and based on this analysis new methods for successful public participation should be developed. The new methods would especially be useful when building public space. Ideally, building public space could even begin in a bottom up way.

PARTICIPATION

Participation is an intrinsic part of democracy, which requires citizen engagement in the decision-making process on a regular basis, not only at the polls. Fostering participation at the local level is crucial: 'the balance between authority and participation may lean more to participation at the local than is the case at the national level' (van Beckhoven 2006: 66).

It is the residents who know their needs, preferences, ideas and emotions, and who wish to live in a pleasant environment (Diers 2006). It is therefore impossible or at least irresponsible to plan a particular urban or rural area without cooperating with the locals.

At present, urban development processes are typically initiated by private developers and investors. In these circumstances, the interests of local residents, who instead of seeking profit seek quality of life, are an important counter-balance to the interests of private capital. Participation of local residents is therefore crucial to sustainable and balanced spatial development.

However, local participation can sometimes turn away from fruitful engagement. Sometimes it is reduced to a so-called *nimbyism*, a process in which local residents oppose particular projects just because they are planned in their local area. In such cases, local participation is often not particularly helpful for local decision makers, but such open expressions of particular interests should still be taken into consideration. After all, an appropriate official response and convincing arguments can still help in the development of the project and raise the level of trust in the institutions.

APPROACH RATIONALE

History

When discussing local participation in the case of Slovenia, its historical perspective should certainly be analysed. During the 1970s and 1980s so-called self-management socialism was developed, which involved an extensive amount of top-down citizen involvement with very limited effect on actual decisions. Such participation was often even planned to exclude people from the decision-making process (Ploštajner, Černič-Mali & Sendi 2004: 21). In effect, the decades of self-management socialism had negatively affected the interests of citizens to participate in the formal decision-making process at all levels.

Trust

After the collapse of the self-management socialist experiment, liberal democracy was established in the early 1990s. Even though the expectations about the new social system were set high, many of the 'old system' problems still remained. This applies also to participation in spatial planning, which remained more or less dysfunctional. Nevertheless, the roles of actors in spatial planning changed thoroughly. After the political

and social transition, land ownership became the dominant determinant in all planning and private investors became a decisive agent in the process. Consequently, local communities were limited when trying to plan their local development according to the common interests of the local community. Owing to the newly gained power of capital, the dominance of the investor's side in the planning process became tolerated by institutions, and after a while even taken for granted. Eventually, this severely diminished trust in local institutions. Trust in local administration or city government is crucial to functional cooperation between decision-makers and local residents (Stanič 2005: 2); otherwise, participation is perceived as pointless. Grounds for constructive participation are most severely affected by the lack of trust. Consequently, interest in participation among the individuals is very low unless there is a particular plan or project that threatens the quality of (daily) life and thus mobilizes the local community.

Reduced participation

In the case of Slovenia, it could be argued that the level of participation is often reduced to so-called nimbyism or plain opposition (Križnik 2008: 77), which is a form of participation that presents no alternatives, just plain negation of the planned projects.

Interest in participation is usually very low until some new local plans are presented. That might sound quite normal, but what we would like to emphasize is that there is an obvious

lack of proactive participation. Very rarely do communities contact local administrations with ideas regarding, say, how to regenerate a neglected area within their neighbourhood. In general, the level of Slovenian participation causes concern, mainly because there are almost no signs that the amount and quality of participation is increasing. The number of local initiatives is increasing, but this could partly be explained by the proliferation of new development projects. Another part of the explanation could be dysfunctional legislation at the national level: inclusion or participation of the community or public organizations is envisaged after the plan has already been finalized, which strongly limits the possibility of local opinion influencing the plans.

In sum, participation has been labelled as dysfunctional for all the involved parties:
- investors think it prolongs the project preparation. Projects opposed by local residents are often delayed or fail entirely;
- residents feel unable to address or even influence development projects, thus opposition is the main response to spatial planning;
- city administration and government fail to acknowledge and defend public interests or at least to give an impression that they defend public interests, the result of which is a lack of trust in local and national institutions.

POLOK PROJECT APPROACH

The PoLok[1] project was conceived and implemented to address the problems of dysfunctional participation in Slovenia. Specifically, the project aimed to empower local residents so that they become actively involved in planning the area in which they live, by participating in decision-making processes at the local level. The project is based on the belief that long-term spatial planning collaboration of all participants – including residents, local and national administrations, investors and professionals – provides the best and most efficient means of improving the quality of life and meeting the expectations of all parties involved.

The project presented two main tools to improve participatory practices. The first was the model of local partnership, in which local residents, institutions and private actors would work together towards improving the quality of life in a specific area. Key features of such a model were set and partially tested within the project. The second tool was improved networking of local initiatives between themselves and with local and national institutions and expert organizations. A Web platform was established to support networking, but the main activities to facilitate improved networking within the project were seminars and workshops. Seminars offered a wider perspective on the issue of local participation. This involved promoting the benefits of local participation to a wider audience, and disseminating information and knowledge regarding public participation. On the practical level, various workshops were organized. The purpose of workshops was to integrate local initiatives into spatial planning processes at the local level, and to

establish a link between the local initiatives and the city administration in order to improve cooperation between them.

Seminars

The main purpose of the seminars was to promote the benefits of local participation and to disseminate knowledge and information regarding local participation in spatial planning.

The first seminar focused on local initiatives and the general public interested in local participation. The second seminar targeted institutions and professionals dealing with spatial and urban matters. Representatives of institutions, such as local and national administrations, and planning practitioners were invited, though attendance was lower than that of the first seminar. It proved to be rather difficult to deal with the institutions and the response was less positive. Therefore, a high-profile public event was also held in order to promote local participation to a wider audience. This was an English language round table addressing the role of civil society in urban planning, featuring distinguished guests, including the President of the National Assembly and the head of Ljubljana's urban planning department.

Workshops

Workshops were organized in cooperation with specific local initiatives, addressing their direct problems and needs. In the first workshop

Figure 1: The PoLok workshop.

the management of the local traffic situation in a particular Ljubljana neighbourhood was discussed. The results were very satisfying but putting the results into practice at the level of the city administration is so far lacking. The main lesson learned was that at the beginning of cooperation, local residents acted mainly on the basis of individual interests – more street parking places for residents, for example. There was a significant shift noted during the workshop. At the end, people were willing to cut the amount of parking places in order to develop more user-friendly public space. The second workshop was organized in Maribor and was devoted to an initiative for setting up an inter-generational centre in a neglected part of the city. Collaboration between the local initiative and relevant institutions working on the same topic was established and future steps agreed to, but a few very important institutions were absent from the workshop.

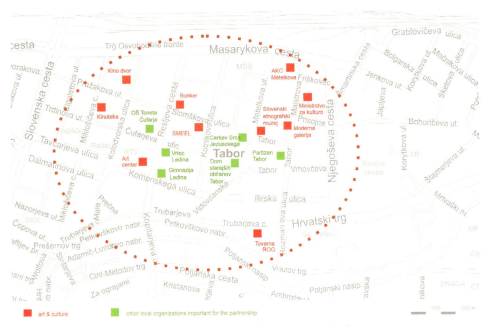

Figure 2: Map of the key stakeholders in the cultural district partnership (drawn by Tanja Maljevac).

Figure 3: The closing conference.

The next workshop focused on the principles of a successful spatial plan for a village in the Karst region. The workshop's main outcome was a commitment made by municipal officials to organize consultations with local communities regarding the municipal spatial plan. The last workshop focused on a local partnership seeking a cultural district in the eastern part of Ljubljana's city centre. The potential of a local partnership involving local initiatives, city institutions and potential developers was discussed. As already mentioned, the concept of local partnership was one of the key tools developed and promoted within the PoLok project in order to increase local participation.

Final conference

Project results were summarized at the final conference. A round table was also organized. Guests agreed that the national legislative framework does not adequately emphasize participation in spatial planning, but that this fact is no excuse for not participating informally or for the passive position of civil society organizations when dealing with spatial planning.

CONCLUSIONS

The level of public participation in spatial planning in Slovenia is low, which should concern local and national planners and professionals. Because of distrust, negative past experiences and untransparent procedures, people have lost faith in institutions, politics and professionals dealing with spatial matters. The result is that people are no longer willing to participate in spatial planning unless they feel threatened by an impending plan or project. Therefore, most Slovenian participation is focused on opposing particular projects, mostly at the local level. The PoLok project addressed the phenomenon of local participation in Slovenia, theoretically and practically. The theoretical part stressed the importance of participation and analysed local participation in spatial planning. It concluded that there is a great need for more and earlier participation in spatial planning processes and more transparent procedures, and that the gap between institutions and local initiatives could be described as very wide and thus harmful to spatial planning in general. It would be naïve to expect the situation to change quickly. Trust is regained only over time, but even so, immediate actions are required, especially by professionals, institutions and city officials.

Perhaps an opportunity to stimulate local participation could include low profile spatial interventions aimed at regenerating neglected public space at the neighbourhood level.[2] It would be a win-win situation for planning public space, because local residents would not only participate in the planning process and influence implementation, they would also identify better with the neighbourhoods and perhaps even take part in caring for public places.

---

[1] The acronym PoLok comes from the Slovenian words 'podpora', meaning 'support', and 'lokalnim', meaning 'local'.

[2] People are usually more emotionally attached to spatial issues on the local level, therefore, it would make sense to foster participation on the local level.

III. / PUBLIC IN PLACE

Kathy Madden

CREATING SUCCESSFUL PUBLIC SPACES

'It's hard to design a space that will not attract people. What is remarkable is how often this has been accomplished.' William H Whyte, author of The Social Life of Small Urban Spaces.

Whyte made this comment as part of a discussion at our office about why good public spaces were not being built more often, given the research that we and others have done concerning why some spaces are well used while others are not. In 1975, when Project for Public Spaces, Inc. (PPS) first started, our mission was to apply what we and Whyte had learned about the use of public spaces in cities throughout the United States. We were convinced that the information we had learned was so clear and easy to grasp, that after our initial three year foundation grant was completed, the need for our organization would simply cease to exist. The design of public spaces would grow out of a deep understanding of how people use and perceive the places they used.

But we were wrong. There are still public spaces built today that are empty and lifeless examples of what *not* to do, which makes us even more convinced that it will require a major campaign to effect change in the way that public spaces are designed.

In its book 'How to Turn a Place Around', PPS outlines eleven principles for creating great public spaces which, it turns out, are pertinent to the essays and case studies that are described in this chapter. One important and overarching principle is 'You are creating a Place - not a Design'. In contrast to the traditional design process, a place oriented approach is broader because creating a 'place' depends more on how the space is managed and requires the involvement of many different disciplines because of the complex issues that need to be addressed.

The principle, 'The Community is the Expert' relates to the importance of the citizens view as the basis for creating good public spaces. In the following essay, Elisabetta Fanti and Anna Spreafico describe how an organization, *esterni,* has used a variety of guerilla interventions and impromptu events to create what, they call, a cultural project and 'philosophical movement'. By focusing on a problem that is important for the future of a city but that is not being dealt with by anyone, (e.g. the emerging Chinese community in Milan which was not well integrated into the life of the City), they create opportunities for citizens to get involved in their communities in a new way. The *esterni* projects also reflects one of the most important yet difficult to achieve principles, 'Start with the Petunias' which refers to the need for short term experiments as a way to begin to effect change in communities.

Three PPS principles for creating good public spaces, 'You can see a lot just by observing', 'Form supports Function' and 'Triangulate' (locating elements in a way that greatly increases the chances of activity occurring around them) are all reflected in the *Tool box for increasing spatial capacitation of public space*, by Sabine Guisse, an architect. Guisse writes that factors such as the way a space is laid out and the way that specific elements are located impact how that space will be used – or not used! She uses words like 'spatial hooks' (e.g. a bench, a row of trees, a shop or a curb) to describe those elements that, if used effectively, can encourage people to use a space in a certain way. If designers learn to understand how these elements relate to people's positive interaction with each other and with the space, they will be able to make better design decisions and the result will be better public spaces. She encourages designers and planners to start by observing how spaces are used and then to develop design concepts that reflect the results of those observations.

How an understanding of the use of public spaces can impact design decisions is also described in *Retracing public space*, by Giordana Ferri who says that before thinking about *what* to design, it is necessary to ask *how* to design. Ferri suggests that if the goal is to make it possible for citizens to have a say in planning, we need to put in place practices that allow this to happen. She also questions what the designer's future role should be both in terms of involving citizens and also in using their knowledge to develop a design that will encourage people's interactions with each other in the space in the future. The essay entitled *Renovating a public space; what next* by Judith le Maire, reflects the principle 'You're Never Finished' or the importance of managing public spaces once they are built. In response to a citizen protest against a government plan for a public space in Brussels and following the completion of a new design for the space, the 'Place Flagey Standing conference' and The Flagey Platform were developed to bring forth residents ideas for managing the space and in planning the future activities that would occur in and around it. The principle 'You can't do it alone', or the need to have partners, is reflected in the essay entitled *Children's imagination and the shaping of urban spaces* where Chantal Vanoeteren discusses the Human Cities educational program which focuses, in this essay, on workshops that involve multiple partners including children in the planning of their urban environment.

It is clear that public space planning is really a 'science' that can yield important data to inform both the design and management of public space. The challenge remains how to bring this science into the mainstream so that designers, people in government and others who make decisions about public space respect and use this knowledge in their work. Only then, will public spaces achieve their full potential to positively impact the lives of citizens in every community around the world.

AUTHOR / Sabine Guisse

CHAPTER / A tool box for increasing spatial capacitation of public space: design and renovation geared toward use

INTRODUCTION

Since 2006, we have observed the use of Brussels public space to better understand how space and individuals interact. In the manner of *sociologie pragmatique* (Boltanski, Dodier, Latour, etc.), we are interested in the shared role of subjects and objects in the use of space. As architects, we focus on the spatial side of this relationship and its consequences: how do people react to objects in public space? We have analysed visual data (individual expressions, forms of interaction, a space's particularities) and the potential of designed elements to equip or force people to use public space. We have also identified some design procedures to improve the capacity of a place to act as a tool, and not as an obstacle, for most public space users. This paper presents one of the products of this research: a tool box, in the form of a book, whose objective is to make use the central criterion for designing and outfitting public areas. It equips public space design professionals to observe the use of places and incorporate what they learn in their design work.

The usage of public space can in fact be facilitated or restricted by a variety of factors.

One of them, spatial layout, particularly concerns design. Spatial *capacitation* and *decapacitation* are propensities of spatial elements to support or hinder user practices. Every isolated spatial element is inclined to be *capacitating* and *decapacitating;* which one depends on the circumstances of use and/or the user. For example, a short wall can be a place to sit but also an obstacle; an exhibiting place can delight, but also trouble the user, etc. Modelling and organizing such elements in space design or renovation involves responsibility of the designer towards the user: transformed places will accept or stimulate some usages, but will also threaten or neglect other ones. Considering that urban public space users are highly diverse, the aim is to maintain or improve the range of possibilities for use. This strategy could cater to multiple uses and offer alternatives to decapacitating situations at the same time. Moreover, a public space opened up to multiple uses can fulfil the unique potential for social experience, and consequently mutual recognition and learning.

Our tool box helps adapt the design and outfitting of public spaces to the reality of their uses as they occur in the field. The tools

can be used by designers (architects, urban planners, urban furniture designers) or those working upstream (programmers, authorities) who also influence the function and/or shape of transformed or newly created public places. The tool box invites producers of public space to add to the project by observing the way space and use actually interact. We have experimented with the tools by providing them to students learning architecture, public space planners and designers. They inquired about the uses of a district's urban places (streets, roundabouts, crossroads, land such as parks or wasteland) to inform their reprogrammation and design exercise. The result was a series of mini-projects, modelled and organized in the local space on the basis of observation and with the help of conception procedures. These tools can benefit the designer who uses them to better understand the influence of space on individual behaviours, which can help him target his spatial intervention; and the user whose practices directly inspire renovation that generates more possibilities for use.

The tools are used one after another in the project process: advice for considering public space in terms of its uses, keys to analysing data, procedures and a catalogue to accompany the design phase. The first tools can be used continually in a relatively independent way while wandering through the town. Initially, the producer of space observes and deciphers how the existing spatial configurations promote or limit uses. Next, he can make use of prospective tools, which help him imagine how the project could intensify the area's *spatial capacitation*, or in other words, increase its possibilities for use.

OBSERVATION

The first tool, 'advice for observation', invites the designer (and also the planner) to analyse how spatial configurations influence the way the space is used. The recommended technique is field observation, which provides an idea of all the 'physical' details of use: the position of people and objects, postures, attitudes and spatial details. The investigation deals with the immediate, tangible conditions of interaction. This kind of exploration is meant to complement analyses of public space use that focus on physical entities: people (social sciences) or objects (technical sciences).

In order to understand use in its purest expression, the observer should be discreet. He does his best to record the situations of use that he observes by means of notes, sketches, photographs or videos. In fact, the instant of use may be very short, and it takes place in an urban environment that is often complex and dense. The field to be observed is the *space of public use*. The observer identifies spatial

elements with which the user interacts: the *spatial hooks* that he sees, smells, touches and hears. Thus the field is not linear or constant. It varies, expanding or shrinking with the user's aptitudes and size, but also with urban morphology (dimensions, proportions and shape of buildings, infrastructure, relief, etc.). If we decide to use a site for a particular project, an observation zone should be defined. This of course must always include the project area, but it should also go beyond that, because users are mobile and move in a network of public spaces. This means that there must necessarily be connections between uses of nearby places: local habits, flows between functional poles, complementarity, conflict or continuity between functions or atmospheres, etc. Finally, no matter how much time can be devoted to the observation stage, moments must be chosen when the circumstances of use vary: the space is crowded or deserted, day or night, good and bad weather, working days and weekends, and so on. This will substantially enrich the sample of uses observed in the same space.

ANALYSIS

The second tool, 'keys to analysis', helps extract and classify pertinent information from the multitude of details of use observed; this is the information that could be reused for the project. We recall that the idea is to understand the tangible influences exercised by space on use. By being attentive to what the user approaches, touches, brushes up against, looks at, follows and avoids, one can pinpoint elements in the

environment that intervene in use because of their form, texture, dimensions, function, etc. These are referred to as the *spatial hooks* of use: pavement, a post, a bench, a row of cars or trees, a lawn, a shop, a curb. Then the observed use is classified according to the type of interaction that occurs between the space and the individual. According to our Brussels case studies, they seem to relate essentially in nine different ways. Consequently, we have created a typology of use in the form of a series of *spatial interaction figures*: Magnet, Shelter, Stage, Sign, Constriction, Bath, Knocker, Breakthrough, Vagueness. Each of these is associated with a particular way that the *spatial hook* and the user mobilize each other during use. To identify the *interaction figure* that is being observed, one simply has to ask what the user and the *spatial hook* are doing to each other. The *catalogue of interaction figures* illustrates these various *interaction figures*. This is a series of photographs taken over years of research, presenting a large quantity and variety of situations of use classified by *figure*. Each figure also has a *script*, which is a description of a whole series of typical repercussions, *capacitating* or *decapacitating*, that this type of use has on the user.

The question brings us to assessing the situations observed, in addition to classifying them. This stage is indispensable to any tool box that is meant to be prospective. But it is also very delicate. In fact, in this public environment, where a variety of users come with his/her own personal aspirations, which are often contradictory, how can one judge which service provided by the space for a given use is good or bad? The principle is that the assessment of the premises is not conducted on the basis of absolute criteria of an aesthetic or technical nature (effectiveness, embellishment, harmony, etc.), which often govern the assessment of space. Nor can social or moral criteria (security, conviviality, encounters, mixing, etc.) be used to assess the situations observed, as this presupposes a judgment of individual behaviour. The assessment is based on the use itself: by detecting signs of *spatial capacitation* or *decapacitation*. At this specific time, does this space restrict or help the user who is being observed? Other keys to analysis are available: *scripts* associated with *interaction figures*, and a series of *behavioural signs* that indicate the user's comfort or unease. Does he reach out to or recoil from objects? Does the person stroll quietly among them? Or, conversely, does he draw back, get jittery, or avoid them? Does he look around inquisitively or anxiously, look away, seem concerned or stare at nothing? Finally, the diagnosis of the place observed is made on the basis of what the space has prevented and permitted among users during a succession of micro-situations. Clearly, this diagnosis is partial. The objective is not to reach an absolute, definitive and closed judgment on any given space. On the other hand, it can help a designer include a certain number of local indicators for use in his project and take a position on pre-existing uses with greater awareness. This kind of diagnosis can also directly add to the project by means of one last series of tools that are described below.

DESIGN

The designer modifies the users' microcosm with his project that maintains, displaces, transforms, eliminates or creates certain *spatial holds*. The final objective of the tool box is to guide the modelling and layout of *hooks* in order to intensify *spatial capacitation* of the area. The last four tools are 'four design procedures' that help a designer integrate the lessons learned from his observations.

The first procedure, *recognition*, is a preliminary. It consists of turning the situations observed in the field into resources for the project. Photographs taken on the premises are classified by *interaction figure* to constitute a sort of *local catalogue of interaction figures*. In addition, the uses observed are plotted on the map of the project. The map and the catalogue are used as a basis for the implementation of subsequent procedures. Consequently, from the outset, the project is linked and open to prior uses of the premises, which at least some users will necessarily perpetuate after the renovation. However, the project for *spatial capacitation* is not reduced to maintaining the conditions of existing use; it targets allowing other uses, exploiting new space, inviting new users who to date could not find their specific place or perhaps any place at all in the space as it exists.

The second procedure, *pluralization*, invites the designer to diversify the *spatial hooks* to increase possibilities for use. With a varied selection of *hooks*, individuals have an opportunity to modulate their uses in

keeping with their culture, age, capacity, mood, desire, etc. The project at first proposes uses according to some kind of continuity: diversifying the types of *hooks* (varying the style of a street lamp, the type of tree, the shape of a bench, the purpose of a building, and so on) while activating the same *interaction figure* as the one that has already been observed. The designer will therefore imagine another scheme that continues to present the user with a Stage, a Knocker, etc. He can imagine it, but also take inspiration from the *spatial hooks* in the *catalogues of interaction figures*: either the *catalogue* made on the basis of local data, in order to multiply *hooks* that already function in the neighbourhood, or the *catalogue* provided in the tool box to import 'new' *hooks*.

For *pluralization*, the project can also propose alternative uses, rather than continuity. The next procedure, *articulation*, helps offer 'inverse' opportunities for use, particularly to respond to situations of *decapacitation*. This is one of the major principles of the *spatial capacitation* project: not necessarily condemning *spatial hooks* when they make certain users uncomfortable, because generally they turn out to be a tool for other users. Instead, we try to develop a system of multiple *hooks* in nearby space that allow diverse uses to coexist in the same place. To offer a targeted alternative for uses that are spatially *decapacitated* or simply not *capacitated* in the existing *interaction figure*, the designer can use the complementarity of six pairs of *figures*: Stage and Shelter, Magnet and Shelter, Breakthrough and Knocker, Bath and Constriction, Vagueness and Constriction, Vagueness and Sign.

Finally, the *extraction* procedure entails identifying unexploited human and spatial potential in the context of pre-existing uses before renovation. Exploitable spaces to which access is prohibited and/or is cut off (construction sites, vacant lots, infrastructures, etc.) are identified along with their potential for public use. Users who can access the site but do not use it (e.g. office employees, elderly persons) are identified by means of statistics and interviews. Extended interviews can sometimes shed light on any spatial reasons for their absence from public space.

CONCLUSION

Basing design on observation of uses is an enriching practice, but one that is long and complex. The succession of observed user bodies gives rise to a particular formulation of spatial opportunities and constraints encountered for a use. The user generally is not aware of this as such, so it is spontaneous, unformatted and outspoken. Both plural and disinterested – this is the potential 'public' expression of what this space allows or disallows regarding uses. Recorded for an 'observant' design, this formulation can act as the 'voice' of a sample of the first public to use this space. It ensures a certain multifaceted representativeness that corresponds to the common dimension of public space whose future is determined by a renovation project. This design practice equates ordinary citizens who 'live' in public space through their uses with ordinary citizens who 'talk' about public space in their proposals and demands in participatory meetings. This 'polyphonic' formulation develops from the multiple uses of a public space by any given user, at any given time. For public space that is open and subject to continually fluctuating uses, this means that the formulation is never over. The assessment of public space from the standpoint of uses is not exhaustive, because it is always limited to the observer's time and field of observation. Finally, it should be noted that this expression disclosed by bodies and not structured by any discourse is not a consensus or mediation – it is rough. Observation provides the designer with complex, and often contradictory, information. For these reasons the tools for 'observant' design, as we have developed them, do not provide a ready-made solution. They are not presented as a cure-all for spatial prescriptions. They necessitate a commitment by the designer, and, in exchange, they leave him much room for creativity.

AUTHOR / Giordana Ferri

CHAPTER / **Retracing public space**

INTRODUCTION

This paper presents the description of a public space design project realized in a municipality near Milan, Locate di Triulzi. The case presents an opportunity to determine the role of design by reflecting on the relationship between public space and the experience it engenders.

What is the nature of public space today? How is it perceived and used? And how does physical space relate with public life and encounters between people? Or rather, what form does the public life of people take and what relationship is there between public life and the urban space that supports it?

Lets start with an assumption: the characterization of an urban public place is not only physical but also and above all provided by the sense of belonging of people to that place, namely the ability to link these places to meanings that are not only symbolic but also social and linked to everyday experience.

It often happens that the city's public spaces that are not the result of a historical process or common experience are perceived as

foreign, alien or as sites of transit, mainly because they are not experienced or lived. The historical city itself, consisting of spaces that were once heavily populated by businesses and imbued with specific values, rarely offers places that can be recognized as collective resources or accessible places to live.

It is from this perspective that we will examine, through the case presented below, the theme of public space and its design: public space seen as a resource in the phenomena of interaction, as a platform transformed by negotiated use and the direct intervention of its users.

From this perspective, even before thinking about what to design, the question of how to design arises. If we want to make possible and systematic those moments of interaction that allow users to have a say in planning, what practices must we put in place to encourage people and groups to take advantage of public space and to enhance it and recognize it as such? What initiatives stimulate users to ask: Is this site available for use? What can I do in this place? What can I do with others? How can I share this resource in a way that responds to my personal needs and

simultaneously to the collective need to keep these areas of the community blooming?

This interpretation of public space not only takes into consideration its traditional definition, i.e. a common space that concerns the community; it also originates from and is stimulated by the emergence of major social phenomena to whose development public space is crucial.

This vision springs from the realization that more and more people and groups today express a strong willingness to intervene directly and pragmatically concerning the resources the city offers in order to broaden their scope and enrich city life with activities and initiatives that are made sustainable by the community.

It is as if an important part of our daily life – and its sustainability – depended heavily on relationships that are based not only on a shared feeling, but on a shared doing, on actions related to the construction of mobile and flexible systems that make everyday city life sustainable, more accessible and safer.

In this complex web of requirements, ranging from the need to interact and share life styles, tackle common problems in a sustainable way and experience the city intensely, what is the designer's contribution?

Design has always anticipated and outlined ways of life by offering insights into future reality – intuitions which often encompass a core of values and primary structures that are much more complex than the solutions themselves. Returning to public space, we thus understand that the designer's mission is to reconfigure its use from what has already been made to happen there.

The designer's intervention begins long before he begins the physical design. First he establishes a preliminary framework that 'makes things happen' by linking the place with people. By experimenting with the potential of this interaction, facilities and physical support for the repeatability of events, activities and experiences are designed. This phase precedes the physical design of space distribution, which at this point bases itself on a previous profile of use, on background knowledge about the space, and on the construction of community-wide recognition of it.

It's like when a spontaneous footpath is created in a field, a 'mule track', a short cut formed by the continuous passage of people. This new intervention in public space is led by a strong and silent will to find the best route. It is a negotiation between the existing space and the people inhabiting it, who collectively agree to implement change. It is in this context that the designer must act by developing the idea or, more precisely, bringing about new paths through the placement of physical stimuli.

As we have said, design has always had to precede and envisage new ways of life, and it does so even now, but the horizons in which it exists have expanded and encompass interaction systems. This does not mean that there is no novelty;

on the contrary, something fundamental has changed: the reality that surrounds us. The shift from a product-led society to one led by services provides system design its new scope.

With regards to public space, this approach assumes particular importance today because it can intervene at a level of design that strongly favours the relationship with the user – a relationship aimed at providing autonomy, as design has always done – and the potentials of existing social reality.

Public spaces have to transcend their static nature and become a fluid network of paths that link not only places but people. They must become places 'on demand', perceived as nodes in a system of connections in which, through strong community interest, various occasions might develop.

Taking these considerations as our starting point, the case study presented here is an example of the collaborative construction of public space.

COLLABORATIVE CONSTRUCTION OF PUBLIC SPACE

In March 2009, the old milk plant of Locate, a small town in the province of Milan, was converted into a community centre. The new site was intended to accommodate the new public library, a 200-seat auditorium and spaces for community services and local association activities. The building is in a convenient location: near the train station

and town centre, which has recently seen some major residential development, and accessible from the town's main walkways.

From the start, the city council decided its main goal was to make the centre a vibrant space, a point of reference for the entire community, a place that could sustain itself economically. The first step towards this goal was to involve all local associations in the management of the centre's construction.

The Indaco Department of the Politecnico di Milano and Esterni[1] were called upon at this early stage to investigate and analyse every aspect of the city council's requests. They invited any interested group to the project, became acquainted with them, and proposed strategies and interventions that highlighted the potential of the new multipurpose centre, housing services and the possibilities for future management.

In particular, the objectives to be achieved were:
- to build the identity of the centre as a single entity and not as the sum of its parts;
- to design the coexistence of all the entities present in the centre and the joint management of internal services;
- to decide which community service projects to jointly develop.

After a first analysis of the activities of those involved and a preliminary meeting, it was immediately clear that the resources in the field were very valuable and could offer an interesting variety of activities. However, the individual identities of those involved were

Figure 1: The first association workshop.

Figure 2: Defining a common weekly association schedule.

very strong, and no one saw themselves as part of a single brand new structure. Up to that moment, they had imagined that each would move into the centre but continue its activities independently, sharing the keys at most. This was a problem that had to be addressed immediately for two important reasons. First, because continuing to act independently would greatly reduce the possibility of building a common area capable of offering its citizens new services, meeting opportunities and activities. The second reason was that the building did not have enough rooms to house everyone in separate spaces. This discovery led us to slightly adjust our initial draft to focus the first part of the work on building a common identity that recognized the value of the individual associations. The design work was done during three workshops.

Workshop 1

The first workshop, which was attended by representatives of 15 associations and the head of the library, developed the following themes:
- A common name: the first simple, but symbolically important, step was choosing a common name that would represent the centre and its aspirations for the town of Locate. This was done via brainstorming.

- Map of characteristics: we worked on a common identity, starting from the specifics of each association's work. By classifying their activities we created a map that grouped together all the services offered by each association, as if they were organized into a single entity (Figures 1 and 2).

We then organized all activities into a hypothetical monthly schedule, with times and spaces to be used. This preliminary work allowed us to demonstrate that all the activities of the associations could be carried out at the centre, that the definition of a common programme enhances the experience of the individual and can offer citizens a more attractive programme, and that the centre could remain open daily from morning to night, thanks to the presence of the associations. At this point it was clear to all that the centre would be a valuable resource if used by several partners and interpreted as a vibrant space open to more businesses.

This awareness and new perspective paved the way for the genuine involvement of associations and launched the planning itself. The tools we designed for this phase allowed us to facilitate the process of involving association members and to establish the foundation of the project.

Workshop 2

The second workshop sought to understand how to manage and organize non-receptive spaces and how to share tools. Mainly, we worked on how to divide the space according to 'actions' and not associations, thus key functions were identified, such as: meeting, chatting, storing documents of each association, giving a buffet, conducting an interview with a volunteer or with a member in a quiet place (Figure 3). For this phase, visualization tools were used that allowed us to quickly define the main activities to carry out in the spaces provided. The result was a preliminary draft for a flexible space, divided and usable by all and furnished with tools (printers, projectors, etc.) that none of the associations could have afforded individually. The second workshop was concluded with the definition of activities and roles required to manage the centre, for example: who would manage the calendar and with what means,

Figure 3: Sharing spaces by actions.

who would open and close the centre, who would be responsible for communicating maintenance problems to the municipality, etc.

Workshop 3

At this point the group perceived itself as a union. The third and final workshop proceeded with the design of services.

From this part of the design process the first service projects designed and managed by associations emerged.

The first services that we decided to make were aimed at promoting the centre:

A joint website: to promote centre events and activities, to collect subscriptions and post availability, to provide a forum

for uploading contributions (photographs and texts) and as a tool for streamlining organization among centre members. Weekly information stand: to be set up weekly at the centre's main entrance, to communicate and explain planned activities, answer questions of those who would like be involved in volunteer activities; this is managed on a rotation-basis by the associations.

Biannual event: aimed at engaging citizens in an initiative that allows anyone to propose new activities for the centre, thus enhancing skills within the guidelines established by the associations. This could take the form of a day of celebration when each participant is able to try out their own initiative (a free lesson, performance, etc.) and verify the level of appreciation from citizens. This would allow everyone to feel that the centre is an open space for creativity and allow associations to increase the number of volunteers and activities. Temporary café: to be set up during the events in the auditorium, a 'bar' service that offers a limited amount of easily stored pre-packaged products, possibly fair trade or 'short chain'. This service would enhance the centre's reception and ambience for guests, who would be able to stay behind, chat and get to know each other.
A cocktail night for associations: an event that allows associations to get together and learn more about each other. This event could be organized on a regular basis, for example,

LA SANTORIO
Spazio delle idee

Prossimi passi: idee

1 Sito comune

Sito web

Promuovere gli eventi e le attività del centro, consentire la raccolta di iscrizioni e disponibilità, mettere a disposizione un forum sul quale ognuno possa caricare contributi foto e testi. Avere a disposizione uno strumento web per rendere più efficiente l'organizzazione tra i soggetti presenti nel centro.

2 Banchetto informativo

Banchetto in biblioteca

Presentare settimanalmente le associazioni con un banchetto informativo all'ingresso principale del centro per comunicare i loro programmi, spiegare direttamente la loro organizzazione e rispondere ai quesiti e le curiosità di chi vorrebbe essere coinvolto in un'attività di volontariato.

3 Evento semestrale di richiamo

Ricerchiamo esperti in...

Coinvolgere i cittadini in un'iniziativa che consenta a tutti di proporre nuove attività per il centro valorizzando le capacità di ognuno secondo gli indirizzi indicati dalle associazioni L'iniziativa potrebbe concretizzarsi in una giornata di festa nella quale ogni proponente ha la possibilità di organizzare un numero zero della propria iniziativa (lezione prova, esibizione...) e verificare il livello di gradimento da parte dei cittadini. Questo consentirebbe a tutti di sentire il centro come uno spazio aperto alla creatività di tutti e permetterebbe alle associazioni di arricchire il numero dei volontari e delle attività da proporre.

Ricerchiamo...
persone che hanno voglia di proporre attività nell'ambito della cura di sé, dell'alimentazione...

4 Presenza in eventi mensili

Eventi nell'auditorium

Offrire durante gli eventi nell'auditorium un servizio "bar" limitato a prodotti confezionati e facilmente conservabili, magari del commercio equo o di "filiera corta". Questo servizio qualificherebbe l'accoglienza del centro e renderebbe più gradevole la permanenza degli ospiti, i quali avrebbero modo di conoscere meglio le attività e le realtà presenti.

5 Aperitivo

Aperitivo delle associazioni

Proporre momenti di aggregazione finalizzati allo "stare insieme " e all'incontrarsi. Questi eventi potrebbero avere una cadenza costante, per esempio un sabato su tre, in relazione alle risorse delle associazioni e alla risposta del pubblico. Sono momenti che possono rappresentare l'occasione per i cittadini di avvicinarsi gradualmente alle realtà associative e alla vita del centro.

E ora... ...Spazio alle idee!

abbiamo bisogno anche del tuo aiuto!

Figure 4: Planning common activities and services.

every third Saturday, depending on association resources and public response. These are moments that can provide an opportunity for citizens to gradually become familiar with the associations and the life of the centre (Figure 4). Our work was concluded with a party to celebrate the centre's inauguration and the beginning of all activities. The project continues and is being followed by CIESSEVI, an organization that provides professional support to non-profit associations. During the pilot period, the new network of associations, with the help of CIESSEVI, will try to work out any management issues that arise in the first months of activity.

CONCLUSION

This project has demonstrated how the intervention of designers in public space might induce innovation and create possibilities to develop and optimize public space function. This interpretation of public space featured here focuses on modality of use with the objective of imagining space as a platform structured in relation to the activities it can generate. These spaces thus become alive, open and meaningful. They are nodes in a system where the trajectories of individuals and populations intersect, generating common spaces and places with a new polarity (Figures 5 and 6).

[1] Politecnico di Milano: Ezio Manzini, Giordana Ferri with Lucia Di Sarli; Esterni: Beniamino Saibene, Anna Spreafico with Chiara Monteleone.

Figure 5: Communicating to final users.

Figure 6: The opening.

AUTHORS / Elisabetta Fanti and Anna Spreafico

CHAPTER / *Esterni,* **ideas and projects for public space**

ESTERNI, BASED ON A TRUE STORY

Esterni is a cultural association that develops ideas, projects and interventions, and designs creative solutions for cities and public spaces. Its work is driven by strong tension of ideas, critical thinking and ongoing research.

Esterni was established in 1995 out of the wish of three young students to do something for their city (Milan): a city that did not stifled creativity, youth and culture; a secluded city, unable to invest in the future; a city where public space was (and still is) increasingly the object of private interests and stolen from the citizens.

At first, *esterni* improvised interventions, impromptu events and collective performances; little by little these actions started involving an increasing number of people and coalesced into a cultural project and philosophical movement.

Figure 1: Setting up the Public Design Festival (photograph: Masiar Pasquali).

All the interventions respond to existing problems and are conceived to improve life in the cities and relations among people, and to create new spaces for sharing, socializing and cultural development. Since the beginning, projects have been developed around one main issue: the public space. Over the years, *esterni* has developed a new and innovative discipline, *design pubblico* (public design): design for public space.

DESIGN PUBBLICO: PUBLIC SPACE DESIGN

Public space is where the city recognizes itself as a community, a place for meeting and exchange, cultural and democratic growth, where barriers among individuals are knocked down, where the isolation created by private spaces disappears, where conflicts can be settled.

When public space is not designed, it is not used, and becomes subject to private interests. In Milan (and in Italy), this is a real problem, a true emergency: public space is repeatedly threatened, stolen from citizens, subject to privatization. Public space is often just gaps between buildings.

This is why a movement is needed to liberate, review and design it, to restore it to its proper function and protect it. The city belongs to one and all.

In 2007, *esterni* published a public design manifesto that guides all its projects

in public spaces (past and future):

What is public design?

A different way of experiencing the city.
A design attentive to the ideas of
and services for citizens.
A collective project.
A resistance to urban and
cultural desertification.
A way to rediscover the city's
socializing potential.

An alternative reading of common places.
A practice of utopia in the public space.

CASE STUDIES

Through its interventions, *esterni* aims to raise awareness of urban issues and to promote positive use of public space and a new way of thinking about it. It specifically targets citizens, institutions, designers and architects, since in Milan and in Italy there is not yet a true culture of public space.

Esterni works primarily through cultural projects that can be classified as:
– guerrilla interventions aimed at focusing attention on a specific situation/problem;
– structured and institutional projects that suggest practical solutions to the problems of public space.

Figure 2: A public event in Via Benedetto Marcello: street fairs and urban picnic along the street closed for construction (photograph: Stefano Frattini).

The case studies presented in this chapter illustrate the methodology of *esterni*, which is mainly based on citizen involvement.

Beyond the building site

Project data: *three years, €43,000 budget, one neighbourhood, two building sites*

According to its policy of public space renewal, *esterni* has created the *Beyond the building site* project, a direct intervention at building sites that stands for an ideal model of how to deal with urban emergencies, turning the building site back into a physical and ideal space the city can exploit.

The building site area is no longer closed because of work-in-progress; on the contrary, it progresses towards new opportunities: the work space comes to life, turns into a place where people can meet, get informed and discover the building site itself, all in order to help create a new public square or community.

Beyond the building site is a cooperative project between the construction company responsible for the building site and the people living in the neighbourhood of Via B. Marcello and Via Ozanam, in Milan. The aim is to minimize inconveniences to residents and to create a new community.

Communication

Most of the time, building sites are born without any communication to the people living near the work area. People don't know what is going to happen, how long it will take, to whom they can pose questions, or how to deal with inconveniences caused by construction. The opening of the two building sites in Via

B. Marcello and in Via Ozanam included the installation of large communication banners that continually update work progress; a call centre to tend to requests, suggestions and complaints; and a newspaper, distributed to residents, Containing neighbourhood history, details scheduled construction and techniques, recipes submitted by residents, and news.

Direct interventions at the building site

The starting point is to consider the building site as a lively place that can be exploited by the city. A first kind of intervention concerns the construction site fences, transforming them into a new public space: hanging plants and water fountains, billboards with neighbourly messages, artistic displays instead of advertising posters, raised viewing platforms with audio guides, benches where passers-by can play cards, chat, read or leave a message on a notice board, and additional devices like bicycle pumps and swinging gee-gee.

Residents and shopkeepers maintain all interventions, so they share in responsibility and feel involved with the project and the transformation of their neighbourhood.

China Film Festival

Project data: *two days, €15,000 budget, one piazza, 12 associations involved*

Figure 3: A performance at the building site in Via Ozanam
(photograph: Laila Pozzo).

Milan and many other Italian cities have been enriched over the last few years by the increasingly large presence of foreign citizens. Immigrants from other countries, who are not always part of organized communities, establish groups with well-defined cultural and social identities, and become more and more integrated in the city, in spite of all obstacles and difficulties. These obstacles are sometimes the result of the lack of initiatives dedicated to foreign communities.

In 2007, the well established and sizable Chinese community in Milan is at the centre of a dispute and under attack in the media, resulting in an escalation of tension between the community and Milan citizens.

In June 2007, *esterni* hold the first edition of the China Film Festival, an exploration of high-quality Chinese films, organized in collaboration with Milan Chinese organizations, associations and private citizens.

The two-day festival takes place in Piazza Gramsci, a piazza in the heart of Chinatown. The festival featured open-air screenings of Chinese films (in the original language with Italian subtitles), live concerts by young artists from the Chinese community, a lottery to win a trip to Beijing, and Chinese food.

The aim of the two-day festival is to create a place where Milanese citizens and Chinese residents can meet and have fun, get to know each other and thus overcome obstacles and prejudices.

Esta es una plaza

Project data: *five days, €2,500 budget, 15 students, approx. 30 x 90 m fenced-in empty lot*

In December 2008, *esterni* is invited by La Casa Encendida to hold an international student workshop in Madrid; *esterni* is asked by the cultural centre to intervene in the Lavapiés district of Madrid in a fenced-in empty lot to fulfil new appropriation and functional potentials.

Lavapiés is a multi-ethnic neighbourhood with large numbers of Asians, Indians, North and West Africans and Latin Americans. Located in a central area (close to tourist spots such as Reina Sofia Museum and Atocha Station), Lavapiés is still known as a working class neighbourhood. Bordered by Calle Atocha to the east, Ronda de Valencia to the south, Calle de Embajadores to the west and Calle de la Magdalena to the north, the district has no parks, no areas designed for kids (apart from a very small one in Plaza de Lavapiés) and few public areas.

Activity takes place over five days. Time is too short for a detailed project. A general concept must be defined, tested among residents and implemented in reality. The project is developed through a *learning by doing approach*.

On the first day, after a brief presentation about *esterni*, a brainstorming session immediately begins concerning the plot of land in Calle Doctor Forquet, the fenced-in empty lot chosen for the intervention. Several ideas emerge,

Figure 4: Blueprint for esta es una plaza.

to learn whether these ideas meet resident needs, the students are invited to walk around the neighbourhood, interview residents and debate possible uses of the urban void.

On day two the renewal project is defined: it is decided to transform the lot into a new public *piazza* with a vegetable garden, theatre, park with hammocks and benches, football pitch and badminton court, and a public covered market. The project is called *esta es una plaza*.

The group is divided into two smaller teams: one focused on communication and promotion of the project, the other on researching necessary materials and in-kind sponsorships (as the budget is insufficient for such an ambitious project). A blog is launched at www.estaesunaplaza.blogspot.com, and a first promotional flyer is created. All neighbourhood residents are invited to follow what is going on, to be part of the project and to attend the grand opening of *esta es una plaza*, scheduled for three days hence. Over the next two days all necessary

materials are acquired (pallets, vegetable seeds, hammocks, nails, hammers), the local press is informed, and residents appear curious about what will happen with the lot, forgotten now for more than 20 years.

It's time to enter the urban void and start with the renewal. Unfortunately, the city council, despite what was previously agreed with La Casa Encendida, is still waiting for authorization to enter the site. What can be done? Much discussion take place among the group, and between the group and La Casa Encendida. Late in the afternoon of the fourth day, La Casa Encendida grants permission to enter the site even though the local government has still not authorized it. The gate lock is broken. There is much work to do: rubbish to be removed, soil to be tilled, a theatre to be built...and the inauguration must be organized: there must be music, a play, catering, the opening of the market.

At 6:00 p.m. on day five many people are waiting at the gate. *Esta es una plaza* is ready to welcome everyone. At the end of the night almost 600 people have visited the urban void. Everyone interested in participating in the project and keeping it alive is invited for a meeting the next day at 2:00 p.m.

The next day, approximately 50 residents interested in working on *esta es una plaza* show up. With the help of workshop students, *esterni* organizes a programme for the days to come and leaves Madrid. *Esta es una plaza* is still open. The Madrid City Council has closed it twice, but residents

Figure 5: The abandoned lot before and after taking action, transformed into esta es una plaza (photograph: Pasquale Covucci).

collected signatures and organized public events, such as a public lunch in front of the closed gate, to mobilize the community, with the result of having the urban void back and a new public space in the Lavapiés neighbourhood.

Smile, you're on air!

Project data: one night, €1,500 budget, 100 x 90 cm triangular road signs

Seven days a week, 24 hours a day we are under the control of thousands of electronic eyes in parks, streets, squares, stations and many other public spaces. Every year the investment in video-surveillance rises, under the assumption that more CCTV cameras means more safety for everyone.

How do you feel knowing that everything you do in public space is under surveillance?

Smile, you're on air! is an intervention of public art to spur thought about social control. A guerrilla action is held in a cold winter night of January. Five *esterni* units go all around the city to fix new experimental road signs, similar in size and graphics to real ones but with a different and ironic message, *Smile, you're on air*, just below CCTV cameras in strategic hotspots of Milan.

Figure 6: Smile, you're on air road sign, below CCTV cameras in a strategic hotspot of Milan (photograph: Pasquale Covucci).

CONCLUSIONS

Thanks to these years of projects, research, studies and encounters in Italy and abroad, *esterni* has realized that there is a growing need for a new kind of design for public space. Public institutions, designers and everyone involved in the development of our cities should address the need for a better life in cities, for public spaces designed for the people who use them, and to help them use these spaces.

In Italy, except for some isolated experiences, the culture of public space is not yet born; institutions lack planning ability, and private investors are concerned mainly with private interests and private spaces. Abroad there is a more sensitivity to the design of public spaces, it is often at the top of the political agenda; *esterni* feels the need to bring this awareness to Italy, disseminate information, present new projects and awaken a new consciousness. To this end *esterni* has created the Public Design Festival, a festival completely dedicated to public space and its celebration.

The festival is held in April during the International Furniture Fair, a time of year that attracts Milan professionals responsible for how public space can be conceived. If institutions seem to feel no urgency to redefine public space, at least designers and architects can try to promote the issue. The Public Design Festival is a platform to explore the infinite possibilities of public space and discuss it with professionals and local institutions.

AUTHOR / Judith le Maire

CHAPTER / Renovating a public space: what next?

INTRODUCTION

This article addresses the Standing conference of the citizen of Flagey, an experiment motivated by and serving citizens who wish to prolong their involvement in public space management.

Several factors go into renovating a public space: the space itself, time, the actors and information exchange. Some are more important than others to participants as the value given to each factor depends of the actors (le Maire 2009). Of crucial importance is the value the town planner grants to both physical and human environments. Should the planner start over entirely, he would then treat the project within a space reduced to its own geometry and take the environment into account in a 'scientific' way: geographically, economically, anthropologically, historically. He might even get to know the '*genius loci*' in all its material, physical and human complexity. Eventually, he would increase his knowledge of the environment thanks to what other actors know, then consider the project to be 'located', rooted in that place, tradition and community.

The value granted to the project's temporality is crucial to the success of the comprehensive process. Wanting to know people implies an interest in the past and traditions and thus a necessity to begin consultations in a project's early stages so as to define and conceive them. But it's also necessary to prolong the comprehensive process once the project has been completed, in order to manage it and involve citizens in the occupation of the space.

FIRST PHASE: PROJECT PARTICIPATION AND THE MAKING OF PUBLIC SPACE

In 2003, in order to prevent flooding, Brussels public authorities built a storm drain underneath Place Flagey. At the time, Place Flagey was only considered the drain's 'lid': public space was treated as a negligible element relative to the technical aspect, and the task of building the Place was assigned to engineering office subcontractors without a call for tenders or an architecture competition.

Area and Brussels Region residents, groups, associations, individuals and schools reacted by creating the Flagey Platform, which issued a 'Call for Ideas' that received 180 proposals submitted by local, national and international architectural agencies.

The 'Call for Ideas' attracted the attention of political authorities, who launched an international competition. The winning design was implemented and the new Place Flagey was completed in July 2008.

SECOND PHASE: POST-PROJECT PARTICIPATION : THE STANDING CONFERENCE FOR PUBLIC SPACE LIFE

The idea of a Standing conference was put forward during the protest against the original Place Flagey project. Back then, criticisms and reflections affected the definition of physical urban space but also the things themselves.

The occupancy of the square during and after its inauguration was orchestrated by the city, which agreed to allow an open-air market and the simultaneous possibility to park on the square. Moreover, events were organized and sponsored for advertising purposes, and a large video monitor financed by advertisements was erected.

The Flagey Platform then created the Place Flagey Standing conference, which seeks to involve residents in square management and the planning of activities in and around it. Residents use their knowledge and the expertise acquired during the square's planning and construction to reflect on life within public space.

In city planning, the comprehensive process is based on an exchange of knowledge among the project's actors (architects, builders, citizens). During the first phase, citizens aimed to shape the square project.

Making a citizen equipped with a 'know how to think' technique became an effective approach during debates over the project's conception and execution. Actors investigated competition mechanisms, project selection criteria and Brussels city planning regulations. Authorities were informed of resident expectations, site user experiences and the site's identity as part of the Maelbeek Valley. Exchange allowed the creation of a common language between architects and citizens.

Four selection criteria guided competition judges: city planning and architectural quality, functionality, environmentalism and sustainable development, ability of the architect to communicate the idea to the inhabitants and participation methodology'. The winning architects, D+A and Latz, met

the last criterion by committing themselves to creating a Standing conference. The architects established dialogue with the other actors, recognizing their resident expertise and collective right as citizens to manage space occupation.

The success of the Flagey process was due to its execution over a long period of time that included a first, planning phase and a second, post-production phase. Actors incorporated knowledge in order to prolong the involvement of citizens through an ongoing forum.

STANDING CONFERENCE OBJECTIVES: HAVING A REFLECTION ON LIFE WITHIN A PUBLIC SPACE

The Flagey Standing conference discusses:
- the planning of on-site activities and video monitor presentations;
- public space periphery functions (i.e. housing, shops);
- the programming of other neighbourhood public spaces.

All square and neighbourhood users have been invited to take part in this discussion. Members of cultural, commercial or academic associations also participate.

D+A and Latz's idea for a Standing conference specified the creation of a non-profit organization of citizens and authorities in charge of managing the square, and of which the firm itself served as secretary for two years

after the square's inauguration. A general assembly and an administrative committee have been planned. Final decisions are the responsibility of city and regional authorities.

The Flagey Platform decided first to list the occupations of the square (markets, circus, fair, car park, casual games) and then to ask the residents to suggest activities. From this, the Standing conference suggested a programme '…keeping in mind that it is essential for the square to have an existence of its own in times when nothing is programmed…left to the site users' spontaneity' (Plateforme Flagey 2007).

The 'Flagey permanent Standing conference' was launched during a meeting of city and Brussels Region representatives. The latter initiated the meeting but never published the minutes. Therefore, the Standing conference exists only through local associations. It takes part in opinion-gathering activities and debates over square uses and programming voids in other neighbourhood public spaces. It seeks recognition by legitimate authorities.

YEAR ONE: DEFINING LIFE WITHIN THE PUBLIC SPACE

In July 2009 local associations and Standing conference members organized a workshop on Place Flagey. During the day's festivities, passers-by wrote on paper affixed to the benches bordering the square, posing questions about current square activities, praising or criticizing its management, and expressing wishes for the future.

They requested more frequent cleaning and stricter police supervision of on-square parking. They also praised daily meetings and how the square serves as a playground for children. Negative criticism included the lack of green areas, and controversy over the video monitor: 'Isn't it possible to conceive a public space without advertisements?'; 'This "television" stays on with no cultural or association programming'; 'The city shows films promoting Brussels'.

The Standing conference can communicate its opinion through other Brussels Region bodies, neighbourhood associations, Local Integrated Development Committees set up via neighbourhood contracts (urban renovation) and festivals.

WHAT MODELS FOR THE STANDING CONFERENCE?

Forums for citizens overseeing the creation of sustainable areas throughout Europe are prerequisites for the Standing conference. But in addition to the environmental and economical stakes, sustainable city planning depends on a social pillar based on participation. Citizen forums influence the sustainability of citizen public space appropriation. The pre-existence of committees or groups seems to be a factor in the success of any project's definition and management. They are the primary motivators and organize themselves during development. Examples include Forum Vauban (Fribourg), Kuka and Krokus (Krönsberg), GlashusEtt Environment Information Centre (Hammarby Sjöstad-

Stockholm), the Renovation Centre (Vesterbro), and the Information Centre (BedZED). Many examples and much research show the benefits of post-project resident city planning. ARENE (*Agence Régionale de l'Environnement et des Nouvelles Energies*) holds that, '...the different actors concerned being parts of the project all throughout the elaboration and during the exploitation phases of the projects, as an inseparable element of the sustainable development process, does make a difference. Those examples (of sustainable urban areas) suggest different modes of governance favouring people's expression for a more widely shared management of operations... Beyond the treatment of environmental, economical and sociological themes, the success of the development of these areas also depends on original plans of governance. They are being installed as soon as an operation starts and in a sustainable way, i.e. they're being kept over time' (ARENE 2005).

In Switzerland, for instance, the Coopératives d'Habitation Genevoise (Geneva Housing Co-ops) states that residents are involved in the 'creation and the life of the neighbourhood' by 'taking part in the development' from the beginning and 'in the management' in a second phase (Groupement des Coopératives d'Habitation Genevoises 2007). It further specifies that participation occurs through support structures capable of channelling energies. It offers a neighbourhood forum (taking part in management, encouraging local business, providing information neighbourhood life).

PERENNIAL PARTICIPATION OF BRUSSELS PROCESSES

In Brussels, neighbourhood contract or public space funding ends with the project's completion. A survey of 'socio-economic projects achieved within a Neighbourhood Contracts context' shows the importance of prolonging funding mandates to include post-contract participation.

The SRDU (*Secrétariat régional au développement urbain*) reports: 'An opinion about the conditions for making the projects last and which require to be carried out beyond their funding by the Region... In order for these projects to keep being positively assessed, the aim of that survey is to anticipate the end of the project being funded by the Region and to make Regional, community and Town officials aware of the needs in terms of employment... Each project for generations 2001-2005 and 2002-2006 underwent an analysis and a concertation with the concerned Town services and/or the developers, in order to consider funding possibilities that may guarantee actions to last' (2006).

The SRDU is studying how to 'lead actions of community development through reflections about the creation and the management of common equipments and public spaces'. This survey shows that 'supervision actions for local equipment and public spaces must be heeded first because they must continue to guarantee that new spaces in those neighbourhoods are animated and accessible'. Some public spaces managed by the Brussels environment administration also illustrate post-project management, in the form of permanent surveillance by local groups. This is the case for the skatepark of Les Ursulines. BRUSK – a group of skaters – took part in the project's conception and obtained a contract and annual grant from the environment administration to provide activities twice a week with neighbourhood children. Recyclart is also highly involved, having built urban street furniture for its socio-professional training courses. The environment administration maintains spaces and plants once a week and cleans twice a day. The ongoing mobilization of actors of the initial participatory process guarantees the space's use.

CONCLUSION

Without actor participation in the development and management of their own environment, public spaces are often damaged or left to decay. Creating management groups is recommended in order to ensure sustainability: they prepare themselves for the task through participatory processes. They know the reasons, choices, and objective and subjective variables concerning the development of the place and, therefore, are capable of managing and improving it. They can identify problems and security needs, and knowledgeably discuss proposals for action.

During the first phase of the Place Flagey project, the architect and local authorities shared responsibility with the people who use the site. Authorities were no longer seen as

making decisions with little or no foundation, since the arguments had been debated. This arrangement sustains the material (buildings, spaces) and social (the human community) components of the space during phase two.

A comprehensive process developed over a long period of time allows citizens to become involved. Participants then manage the urban space.

Ambivalence fuels the Permanent Conference. If it could hire an employee, it would work more efficiently, but this requires official recognition. But such an institution mustn't be funded at all costs nor be taken over by politics. Its lack of stability is a problem, yet it's valuable: its unrecognized status has motivated members to remember events, publish documents and promote its existence, to exercise great freedom in imaginative terms and in debates. The Standing conference exists because it appeals to those who actually think about the processes that help the city function. This is one of the intangible activities of Place Flagey.

AUTHOR / Chantal Vanoeteren

CHAPTER / **Children's imagination and the shaping of urban public spaces**

INTRODUCTION

Human Cities is a European cross-discipline project whose partners share their experiences to find the best ways to create and promote urban public spaces and observe how citizens use them. Among the many actors concerned by how to use public spaces, children play an important part. Indeed, these spaces provide them with various places to meet, play and socialize. Moreover, their imagination and their creativity can generate new ideas and contribute to design conception. Over the past few years, people have grown more and more interested in educational workshops, books and other methods for introducing children to urban life and city planning. This paper features Belgian workshops that introduce children to the planning or use of their urban environment. These initiatives contribute to the Human Cities teaching curriculum developed for anyone – cultural activity leaders, teachers, associations or parents – who wants to educate children about urban public spaces.

CHILDREN EXPLORING THE URBAN PUBLIC SPACE

Human Cities focuses on interactions between people and objects throughout the city and on relationships between citizens within their public space. A city provides plenty of places for children and teenagers to explore: meeting places, playgrounds, places of exploration for the youngest or of identification for the eldest. A single place can welcome or express various uses according to the hour of the day and the people occupying it. In her book on planning the areas for children and teenagers,

PRIVATE USE AREAS	
PLACES FOR LIVING (AND RESIDENCE)	house/flat (family's, friends', neighbours') private outside places (garden, yard, balcony...) unique/multiple (separated homes, nannies'...)
A CHILD'S PERSONAL PLACES	his/her bedroom (shared or not) more casual places (sheds, secret places...)
SHARED USE AREAS	
'CASUAL AND OPEN' SPACES	public squares, building entrances, cellars, bus stops, car parks... communication axes: streets, roads, pavement... natural spaces: woods, rivers, fields, meadows...
INSTITUTIONAL, BUILT SPACES NOT SPECIFIC TO CHILDHOOD	shops, shopping centres cultural and sport facilities (museums, theatres, libraries, cinemas, gymnasiums, swimming pools, family leisure parks...) institutions (town halls...) and public services (hospitals...)
INSTITUTIONAL, BUILT SPACES SPECIFIC TO CHILDHOOD	school, kindergarten, university infrastructure and places for training, internships...) leisure infrastructure (holiday centres, leisure centres, local community centres...) child care infrastructure (nurseries, crèches...)

Table 1: Areas to live in and to explore (Genelot 1998).

Sophie Genelot (1998) specifies that as a child grows up, he or she gradually lives in more and more numerous, varied and larger areas. If one considers all the activities performed and all the situations experienced, one ends up with an impressive and detailed list, which the author sums up in a chart (Figure 1). Regarding urban public spaces, she stresses that 'streets belong to everybody' and that in order to make that slogan concrete, everybody must know this and understand the relevance and importance of the possibility to share the use of squares and streets. The author specifies that streets are one of the first public spaces children are confronted with, one of his or her first conquests. They are a framework he or she will have to explore on a daily basis, complex spaces presenting a lot of information. They also scare parents and their children, as they are potentially dangerous. The need to protect and orient children is an important factor and solutions must be found to reassure them but also keep open the possibility for personal development by exploring the streets. Professionals who study these spaces strive to improve their conviviality, providing spaces in which the widest possible array of citizens can socialize.

These observations fuel our reflection as well as that of many educators who are aware of the potential of cities to enable youths to express themselves. This paper briefly explores some of the existing methods to understand their needs in order to awaken children's curiosity or help them express suggestions for city planning projects.

PEDAGOGICAL METHODS TO AWAKEN CHILDREN'S CURIOSITY OF URBAN PUBLIC SPACES. HOW DOES IT WORK?

Several interviews of actors who have already developed or experienced such methods within workshops for children are listed below. Some of these methods are appropriate for larger, museum contexts, while others were precisely conceived in order to make children aware of what is at stake in urban public spaces.

WIELS creative workshops for children

WIELS is a contemporary art centre in Brussels. It is an archetypal urban project: an industrial building converted into a cultural space in a formerly industrial neighbourhood located at the nexus of streets, trains, trams, buses and highways, and that used to be multicultural, dense and poor. In order to get there, children

are directly confronted with urban realities. Its educational programme organizes art workshops every Wednesday afternoon and during school holidays. During these workshops artists deal with various disciplines such as photography, painting, drawing and sculpture. A dozen children between the ages of 6 and 12 meet there to develop their creative talents and sometimes delve into deep reflection concerning cities (Figure 1). According to Frédérique Versaen, who is in charge of youth education and mediation, reflecting on more urban themes is part of contemporary artistic processes. Many contemporary artists find their inspiration in the city, which they often consider a living organism with its own rhythm and characteristics distinct from those found in the country. Frédérique Versaen is aware of this, and organizes strolls with children throughout the city so as to confront them with urban realities. One workshop enabled them to discover the work and video of artist Sophie Calle, which focused on the personal and artistic appropriation of a phone booth. This allowed them to visualize interactions between the artist and an urban object. Consequently, the children could customize a street lamp post by affixing drawings, stickers, inscriptions and other adornments. Once this was done, they were asked to observe the effects on passers-by and any implications. During another workshop, artist Katherine Longly suggested children reproduce their route or their 'steps' through the city on a wooden plaque (Figure 2). This imaginary map enabled them to artistically

Figure 1: Workshop with children at WIELS. © www.wiels.org

Figure 2: A child's work at Katherine Longly's workshop.

visualize how they explored the city by reproducing their various routes, stops and networks (homes, schools, dance class, etc.). Along with these educational workshops, WIELS is also involved in public development projects. They organize meetings between adults and children with local town planning actors, by designing street furniture with artists (Eric Angenot) and local authorities in a close collaboration as part of urban renovation initiatives (e.g., neighbourhood contracts).

Art Basic for Children (ABC)

Art Basic for Children is an initiative of the Austrian artist and cultural philosopher Gerhard Jäger. It is described as a laboratory that focuses on artistic awareness and aesthetic education for those aged four and older. ABC

workshops offer a context for experiences that stimulate and create fresh inputs for contemporary social and educational activities. Primary school children – aged 5 to 12 – are welcome in their studios, with occasional workshops for very young children, from the age of 2½. On certain weekends, ABC opens its doors to parents and children so that they might experience the workshops as a family. The ABC studios are the core business of the organization. These are mobile studios with specifically designed activity stations equipped with books, games and toys, sound recordings, videos and other prepared research materials. Visitors have the opportunity to explore the themes of several workshops, which are organized without any pre-established route between the different modules. People are free to let their own curiosity and interests guide them. The main purpose is to build a personal route, stimulate personal discovery according to one's own rhythm and affinities, and become aware of the process as a whole. These workshops have been conceived to induce self-learning while stimulating and strengthening ties between art and daily life. Books are important tools for ABC workshops. Most ideas are found in books, and are enlarged in order to be used separately and to provide tools to stimulate children's imaginations. ABC has a large library with books on architecture, art, education, etc. They are a mine of information and a valuable foundation from which to tackle new subjects and inform children, teachers and parents of various curiosity levels. As specified by Gerhard Jäger, books can provide emotional stimuli and drive an educational process or

self-teaching; a handbook can be created to go along with the work and target communication between children. Animators work in close collaboration with teachers thanks to their own approach and process. Architecture and design constitute important themes. Working with schools broadens children's artistic and architectural awareness. The final aim is to win the children's trust so they will express their ideas, feelings and wishes in terms of architecture, art or design. The ABC studios are often used for exhibitions and urban festivals (Kunstenfestivaldesarts or BRXLBRAVO in Brussels and Kaailand in Antwerp). Through these events ABC offers a range of creative activities and mobile structures to provide children the opportunity to enjoy and explore their urban environment. ABC also wrote the guide 'City Games - Play in the City', a booklet that presents a selection of 'classical' urban games that have been played by many generations (tag, hopscotch, etc.). These easily organized activities require modest funding and materials and only demand a small area. They are employed according to each individual's inspiration and allow children to play within the public space.

Turtelwings

Turtelwings was created in the early 2000s by two designers, a couple, who wanted to share their passion for design in general and architecture and towns in particular. They lead workshops in schools and museums and organize workshops in their Brussels educational studio on a regular basis. These

Figure 3: Stimulating children's imaginations. © Turtelwings

events have been conceived in such a way as to stimulate children's imaginations and set them free (Figure 3). Thus the couple wishes to develop a space where children can play and move about according to their own desires and the role of activity leaders is confined to stimulating their talents and making new experiences possible via various disciplines: music, literature, writing, cinema, architecture, etc. They seek to stimulate the youngest children's spontaneity and open-mindedness, thus enabling each child to solve problems based on his or her individual skills. With available materials, they can freely interpret the workshop's core idea and give shape to their imagination. There is no good or bad interpretation. A short while ago, Turtelwings launched an urban workshop entitled 'Urban Explorers Club', based on the younger generation's perspective on design and urban planning. It consists of exploratory strolls and

Figure 4: Children involved in planning their urban environment. © K&S

museum and public building visits. The main purpose is to collect children's impressions so as to give them greater visibility and involve them in the development of urban spaces.

Kind & Samenleving

Of the series of initiatives presented in this article, Kind & Samenleving is probably developing the most concrete and minutely planned projects. The main part of its work is directly linked to the public orders that are meant to enrich the reflection on and the development of public spaces and parks where children come to play. It seeks to enrich its knowledge thanks to contacts and exchanges with children. It is important to clearly define the aim of the study and what the public authorities wish to observe from

the start. They often work in close relationship with schools so that they can benefit from the existing structure and pose questions to children aged 8 to 15. They observe them during an exploratory stroll and ask about their uses of and activities in public spaces. Then they get to know their potential needs and wishes. They allow them to speak out and all their suggestions are welcome (Figure 4). Teenagers are more mobile and a single place in the city is not enough for them. Investigators must have the necessary qualities to engage in a dialogue with children and teenagers so as to get to know their behaviours and aspirations. They must demonstrate creativity and open-mindedness in order to adapt to spontaneity. This will help capture and render their many uses and observations of urban public spaces. In some cases, when citizen participation is stressed, they get involved in the project's conception phase and observe and comment on the idea based on a series of models.

Yota/Yes and the urban mediator project: KarAkol

The urban mediator project developed by Yota aims to connect a series of actors who want to contribute to the conception of a city that respects children. It helps children express themselves more, involves them in the planning of their urban space and develops many participatory activities. Their KarAkol initiative is a nice illustration of the Human Cities project. KarAkol is a Brussels snail that leads 10- to 12-year-old French- and Dutch-speaking children on a stroll through Brussels in search of nice places in their neighbourhoods. This digital tool helps children map their favourite places.

AND WHAT ABOUT TOMORROW?

This paper briefly addressed methods and workshops conceived to make young people aware of how they can contribute to the design of urban public spaces. The organizations that were interviewed employ their own methods for stimulating children's creativity and acquainting them with a range of urban uses, readings and actors. They propose different stimuli to help them understand and take part in the design of their urban environment. Most of them work to make public places more suitable to children's needs and uses. Some work with artists in order to spark imagination, while others prefer to be more practical and help children to become involved in the design process of a public space. The Human Cities partnership tries to stimulate actions that favour the involvement and awareness of children and young people in the design and uses of urban public spaces. Several interviews and meetings contributed to the teaching curriculum that will be tested in Brussels during the Human Cities Festival, which will take place in May 2010 as the culmination of the first part of the Human Cities project. Workshops will provide children with the opportunity to enjoy and take part in the exploration of their public space, while a group of professionals will share their experiences with children during a workshop conceived for adults.

IV. / PUBLIC SPACE AS A COMMON GOOD

HUMAN CITIES / Public space as a common good

Lise Coirier

Human Cities as a concept is focused on improving the relationship of people towards the common rather than public space. There are two complementary targets - providing some real empowerment to people and motivating public authorities to develop an interdisciplinary creative process for a better sustainable living in the cities. Design appears, in fact in its process, as an effective methodology and approach for achieving a participative and "eco-activist" model for improving ever-changing but sustainable city developments.

In fact, European cities today face both frightening threats and exhilarating challenges, becoming harder to manage and to understand, while fostering their role as the drivers and hubs of our economies. Not only must they compete in attractiveness, in order to encourage talents —both creative and academic — to move in (or not to move abroad), they also need to create a framework that promotes their human capital, while coping with social fragmentation and sustainability. Human Cities as a project and philosophy is therefore positioning itself towards artifacts and spontaneous creations, which are seen and perceived in their uses, living scenarios as well as in their complex urban perspectives.

Design in the urban context comprises all the artifacts that are related to places and cities environments and are interconnected to their users. It is an ongoing process which challenges the urban dwellers as well as the creative minds in their context of a contemporary city culture and underlines its effects on real life situations and site-specific installations in the public space. Recently described by Richard Thieme (O'Reilly Network) and the Graffiti Research Lab, both mainly active in the United States as researchers, the hacking culture can be defined as "the means and methodology by which we construct more comprehensive truths or images of the systems we hack". This same spirit can be applied to urban interventions by hacking into the existing or re-invented language and codes of the city to create a greater sense of understanding and a connection between individuals. Some past and current initiatives underline this type of "bottom up" policies. The Australian curator Steffen Lehmann is describing them in his exhibition and book "Back to the City, Strategies for Informal Urban Interventions – Collaborations between Artists and Architects". Organised in Newcastle (Australia) in collaboration with Berlin (Germany), this very recent urban lab is full of creative inspiration. All the information is accessible on the website www.slab.com.au. Some other events that caught the attention were the ExperimentaDesign Amsterdam and Lisboa which happened in 2008 and 2009. In its book and city tour in Amsterdam, Scott Burnham stressed the idea of Urban Play working closely with Droog Design organizing the happenings Droog Event 2 as a way to enhance International Unauthorized Collaborations and Urban Interventions. The subtitle of his book is even called "The Amsterdam Route: New Catalysts for Public Play and Interaction in the City" and shows how spontaneous creativity can influence the urban environment and lifestyle. Those initiatives are well developed on the following websites: www.experimentadesign.nl, www.urbanplay.org, www.droog.com and are closely bound to value design as a source of human added value regarding the respect, protection, participation and interaction of the people within a space which is not only public but common to everyone who deal with it. These topics have been used as the main theme within Human Cities' call for entries entitled Places to Be, which was launched during springtime 2009 and succeeded in obtaining around 70 proposals. This call aimed at gathering some creative practices, performances, installations, videos and photographs which are revealing projects enhancing the public space as a common good and a place to improve participation, interaction, as well as the freedom of speech and behaviour. A jury composed of the Human Cities network selected thirty projects presented on the following pages of this book. Half of the projects are videos and photographs, and some of them are real-life objects, installations and urban performances. The international dimension is really strong knowing that the projects came from all corners of the world such as India, Israel, Japan, the United States, Australia, South Africa, the UK, the Netherlands, Spain, Italy, Belgium, France etc.

The chosen projects are also to be presented in the public space in Brussels during the Human Cities Festival from 6 to 16 May. The festival is a showcase for raising awareness of public spaces in Brussels through various events and city interventions. The program of the festival aims at reaching the largest number of people as possible and at fostering public commitment right in the prominent public spaces and through socio-cultural institutions that are running relevant projects in locations such as city squares and gardens, inner-city parks, busy thoroughfares or hidden alleyways, disused industrial sites...

Human Cities Festival stresses the concept of cohabitation as one way of sharing the common space and to attract people to exchange their perception – either positive or negative – about the existing or dreamed 'place to be'. Designed objects and city installations, which are worked out at a city scale, can become, in that sense, visual and symbolic references of our urban and social environment. As citizens, we seem to long for more intense and creative relationships with artifacts – the more sensual and tactile the object, the better. This evolution is certainly due to the ever-changing developments of the digital society and the immaterial world surrounding us. Perhaps celebrating public space as a common good brings us closer to a better quality of environment and everyday life. The misunderstanding of the urban place or the misuse of public space are on of today's major urban challenges, which could be acted upon by perceiving cities as "design labs", a recent concept, which has been promoted at the 12th Jacques Cartier's Workshops in Saint-Etienne (FR) last November 2009. The stakes are to create an innovation platform around urban design in order to accelerate change, to communicate and develop shared initiatives to benefit to everyone. Therefore, the design process itself appears as one possible model for the future – through public panels, workshops, competitions and activism. It also allows for greater human interactions and empowers us to participate in the transformation of our own life environment.

May the Human Cities project, and its future initiatives, be the signal of the emergence of a vivid design and hacking culture in European cities, may it spur a urban regeneration process geared towards our most humane longings, leading to the existence of ever more real 'places to be'.

UN-DER-STAN-DING THE CITY

Federica Zama, Federico Lega
Faenza, Italy

Federica Zama seeks to ensure that the square of Faenza, her native city in Emilia Romagna, Italy, once again fulfils its function as a public place for aggregation par excellence, a function which the Mediterranean tradition, from the Greek agora to the Roman forum, has assigned it. Her video City Lost/City Regained shows a mix of scenes recorded in the city with images from following movies: Before Sunrise (1995), directed by R. Linklater, Columbia Pictures, USA; Nuovo Cinema Paradiso (1989), directed by G. Tornatore, Titanus, Italy; and Roma (1972), directed by F. Fellini, Ultra Film, Italy. 'The resolution of complex city problems is certainly not the prerogative of architecture alone, stresses Federica, although this too must play an important role in the creation or revaluation of spaces and contexts that can encourage, on a psychological level, a climate of hospitality relative to "others", and a general improvement in the quality of life'.

Nicolo Piana
Treviso, Italy

Nico Plana has a fascination with posters pasted on walls in the street, which he photographs all over the world, in all their torn, overpasted, washed-out states. These poetic yet accidental compositions are perhaps the most narrative of all urban artifacts, bringing back memories of events long gone, and testifying of the cumulative interplays of nature and man.

Christopher Patten
Indianapolis, USA

From the Industrial Revolution on, the Sanborn Insurance Company has produced a series of maps to assess property in cities throughout the United States. Because these maps were repeatedly updated since their creation in 1867, they are incredibly valuable resources for uncovering a city's urban archaeology. In a city like Muncie, where a huge percentage of the city's urban fabric has been destroyed, paved over or left to decay, the concept of the Sanborn Map suddenly becomes ironic: that which was created to document a city's expansion is now studied to explore its decay. It is especially interesting when the previous use of a space contrasts dramatically with its current use. Christopher Patten's photograph series 'Picnic' focuses on one site that exists currently as an abandoned gas station. The 1911 Sanborn Map reveals, however, that its former use was that of a small park. Further research identified a former family back yard. To represent this, a 1950s era picnic was performed on the gas station asphalt for one afternoon; on the other site, a 'garden' was planted by a quintessential housewife while her husband mowed the lawn. The project shows that staging an urban performance based on thorough research can raise the awareness about a city or town – places become richer and more valuable as their history is exposed to a contemporary audience.

Cristina de Almeira
Bellingham, WA, USA

The book Site Readings was created by combining bits and pieces of images and texts collected from downtown Vancouver, Canada. The various visual/verbal discourses were deliberately removed from their original contexts (the street) and re-combined into graphic spaces (the book). Through their reconfigured relationships, they draw attention to the social narratives, simultaneous contradictions, and poetic juxtapositions that are part of the pedestrian experience of an urban environment. The conception of this book was akin to the act of walking through a foreign town, when new stimuli and messages overwhelm one's biased comprehension of their surroundings. From this outsider position, the acts of editing and designing become a process for making and imparting meaning through a labyrinth of possible visual/verbal paths.

Petra Kempf
Brooklyn, USA

You Are the City is an interactive mapping tool, presented as a book, that creates a framework for understanding the continually changing configuration of the city. As we engage with cities, we create places through which we perceive and construct our own city. This publication allows one to superimpose various realities in diagrammatic layers to build new urban connections. It consists of 22 transparent sheets that are divided into four categories. One moves through the book in exactly the same way one enters any city: with no specific order. You can arrive by a main street or a secondary road, by plane, car or ship, you can move by walking or use public transportation: the perception of the urban framework is always different, but the whole may be always the same. There are as many interpretations of cities as there are people. It is therefore our participation and engagement that form places in cities. You are the city – the city is you!

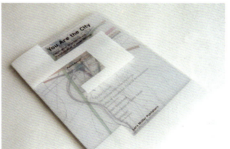

1

2

Orna Marton
Tel Aviv, Israel

Orna Marton's panoramic photography of public spaces, taken around the world, reveals how people and landscape impart a sense of scale and drama to each other and how individuals make their own place in the world. Landscape stands as a metaphor for both reality and territory – both of which are here touched upon and by using panorama as the main technique, simultaneously replicating acts of creation, perception, selection, interpretation and re-composition. The traces of digital processing question the realistic representation of the photographs by turning the panoramic landscape into a patchy backdrop, a synthetic context for the human figure. Time gaps and movement of both camera and subjects in the panorama-making process reveal how body movements transform space into place.

Opposite page, Oma Marton
1/ Picture of "Urban Play", a temporary installation by City Mix group, Bat-Yam biennale of landscape urbanism, Israel, 2008. 2/ Panoramic picture of the Highline, New York, USA, 2009.

Stephanie Carleklev
Braas, Sweden

Stephanie Carleklev's master's degree project explores the possibilities of presenting a city mainly by using sound, thereby triggering imagination and challenging the perception of urban space. In spring 2009, she sound-mapped more than 100 places in the city of Gothenburg, Sweden, at all times of the day and night. The resulting film, called 'About Here' presents nine of them, unmanipulated, together with abstract representations of the places. It proves that sound offers incredible possibilities when it comes to triggering memory, emotion and imagination, while we often rely solely on visual representations. 'When our imagination makes sense out of things, they start to make sense for us. Maybe more important than knowing something is the ability to be curious, to ask questions and even to doubt information' says Carleklev.

Irena Paskali
Köln, Germany/Macedonia

With her panoramic photographs, Irena Paskali tries to show the core designs of urban landscapes and humans living therein in their highest abstraction. By doing this, she questions the nature of objects, attributes or processes and the correlation in which they interact according to our understanding – thereby penetrating into spheres which so far appeared as both familiar and human-controllable. City architecture, e.g. which shrank or are distorted are destroying the illusion of modern humans, to be the sovereign over context, lines of development and over space and time. I enter a metaphysical parallel world, which requests us to a critical reflection of our fundamental ideas in living and raises the question of which material or element the world at all consists. I lift the notional structures of the reality to a new level and undertake the attempt to formulate beside a material, an immaterial entity to show a comprehensive view of reality.

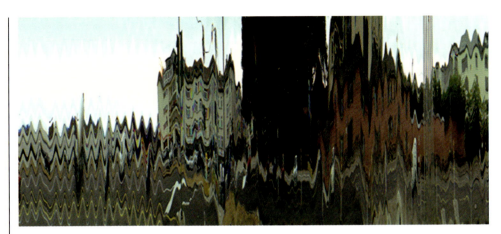

Hana Miletic
Brussels, Belgium

Hana Miletic made a series of seven colour photographs (30 × 45 cm) taken in Skopje, the capital of the former Yugoslav Republic of Macedonia in 2009. Titled 'Skopia', the series refer to the ancient name of the city, which translates as 'watchtower', 'lookout' or 'observation point'. A lookout, or a place from which to keep watch or view landscape, was the photographer's position while making the series, which captures the bizarre position of trees in the architectural structure of Skopje. The city is in a valley surrounded by mountains, which means there is not enough wind to remove pollution created mainly by motor vehicle traffic. The planting of trees downtown could be a measure to improve the city's air quality. Although Skopje does not have enough trees per capita, it has more trees than most large European cities. Skopia is an artist's view of the situation, deeply influenced by the city's ecological reality.

Beate Lendt
Amsterdam, Netherlands

Beate Lendt's 31 minute documentary 'Next21 – an experiment' reveals the unique design process that led to the experimental residential complex Next21 in Osaka, commissioned in 1989 and built in 1993. Driven by the successful cooperation of a group of professionals from several disciplines, the result is one of the only Open Building projects that captured the imagination and remains a fascinating building — which raises questions : What does this project have that others don't? What is its X-factor? Can understanding the mechanisms at work help us create better buildings and thus increase support for sustainability? To gain insight on the X-factor and its creation is what motivated the making of a documentary that could be crucial to the successful proliferation of ecological and sustainable buildings. Because of their age, it was almost the last chance to interview and film individuals like John Habraken, who recently received the Dutch national architecture award for his engaging, future-oriented heritage that today is ever so relevant to our urbanity. To ask the pioneering environmental builders, designers and thinkers about the oil crisis period, and to critically reflect upon their oeuvre and explain their intentions and provide insights into the conditions and mindsets in which this took shape, imparts understanding that will help carry the next wave a bit further.

Swati and Shruti Janu
New Dehli, India

The city is a lived experience. When it comes to Delhi, there is no better way to capture this experience than through its streets and by lanes, where pedestrians and cyclists scurry and dodge traffic and cattle roam amidst blaring horns and screeching brakes. It is this character of the city that Swati and Shruti Janu depict in a fast-paced 4 minute video, through continually changing frames of reference. Delhi is a city pulsing with life, mutating and evolving by the day. It takes in hordes of weary immigrants who manage to make space for themselves in the nooks, corners and crannies of a city bursting at its seams. The film is a journey through the labyrinthine entrails of Delhi, a film saturated with life and that – in a symbolic end – 'spits' the viewer out.

Bendan Cormier
Toronto, Canada

In his 'As Seen By Everyone' video-project, Bendan Cormier aims at describing cities through footage taken from tourist videos posted on YouTube. Videos are sorted by content and grouped with similar videos to create a matrix of simultaneously played visual information intended to recreate a certain atmosphere and reveal certain truths about the space, the rituals performed there, the local tourist economy and the tourists' gaze itself. The first piece, Piazza San Marco as Seen by Everyone is divided into six sequences representing some of the most common and repeated motions, views and actions captured by various tourist cameras: 'Filming Oneself', '360 Degree Pan', 'Pigeon Spectacle', 'Mistakes and Unintended Recordings', 'View from Above' and 'Roaming by Walking through Space'. Similar projects on Tiananmen Square and the Zocalo in Mexico City, currently under production, will highlight common tendencies in the visual consumption of a variety of public spaces around the world.

PAR-TICI-PAT-ING TO THE CITY

Markus Miessen
Berlin, Germany

The author and protagonist Markus Miessen explores architecture, urban planning and the public space. In his book The violence of Participation, he observes : 'Any form of participation is already a form of conflict. In order to participate in a given environment or situation, one needs to understand the forces of conflict that act upon that environment. Just as in physics, a field of forces is defined by the individual spatial vectors that together participate in its becoming, if one wants to participate in any given political force field, it is crucial to identify the conflicting forces at play. Participation is often understood as a means of becoming part of something through proactive contribution and the occupation of a particular role. However, this role is rarely understood as a critical platform of engagement, but rather is typically based on romantic conceptions of harmony and solidarity. In this context, it seems urgent and necessary to promote an understanding of "conflictual participation," one that acts as an uninvited irritant, a forced entry into fields of knowledge that could arguably benefit from spatial thinking.'

Lucile Soufflet
Brussels, Belgium

Lucile Soufflet designs public furniture according to her own vision of the public space in which she puts all her social intentions: her circular, tree-hugging benches in Brussels and Mons, her concrete band, the In & Out, My place, Projet 105 – Peterbos, SDP (Sit Down Please), and her most recent Soft Bench for TF Creation (Saint-Etienne, FR). A range of seven creative and sustainable solutions for cities.

This page, Markus Miessen
1/2/3/ The Violence of participation

Opposite page, Lucile Soufflet
1/ Sit Down, Please. Brussels (BE). 2/ Circular Bench. Mons (BE). 3/ Circular Bench. Molenbeek, Brussels (BE). 4/ Myplace, a project for Anderlecht, Brussels (BE). 5/ Soft Bench for Tôlerie Forézienne (FR). 6/ In & Out, for Urbastyle (BE).

1

2

3

1

2

3

4

5

6

O DA PROVIDÊNCIA

NO CAMINHO DOS DIREITOS HUMA

IGNORÁNCIAESQUECIMEN
TOEDESPREZOAOSDIREIT
OSDOHOMEMSÃOASPRINCI
PAISCAUSASDOSMALESPÚ
BLICOSEDACORRUPÇÃODO
SGOVERNOS

1

2

Association Inscrire (Françoise Schein)
Paris, France

Using ceramics as a medium for human rights development, Françoise Schein has travelled from Brazil to Les Mureaux, France, in order to apply human rights within the public space through the craft and the intuitive knowledge of people from all generations : 'In 2009, in the City of Les Mureaux, 40 kilometres west of Paris, I created a very large and special project with the participation of 200 inhabitants: over the course of one year, we created a huge city map that looks like a monumental tree and whose leaves are made by the population. Each of these leaves include an image and a philosophical statement created by one person. The result, with its variety of styles and ideas, makes this public art work an expression of the public library and media centre it is applied to. It is an interface between the library and the people, the city and its representation. As an artist, I always thought that creating art in collaboration with multiple minds succeeded in creating very singular results that were particularly attractive for the public realm. Historically, art was not only created by solitary artists but by groups of craftspersons led by masters: cathedrals are a great example of this. Ceramic has showed itself the perfect material for mastering very large scale designs with the intimate small paintings of non-professional participants'.

1/Ceramic installation in Rio de Janero

CityMine(d)
Brussels, Belgium

City Mine(d) is a Brussels-based group of activists. They create places for encounters and debate in cities, without asking for money or looking for profit, making them providers of public goods. This might seem unlikely in an economic system organized around professions and profit. Mums and dads of City Mine(d)ers keep asking, 'What is your job?' and 'Who pays your salary?'. Frankly, nobody knows. To find out, two City Mine(d)ers tested the job market for public goods providers in Berlin over a two-week period. A daily blog kept track of their quest and shared stories about employment in Berlin. A brief documentary resulted from the research, documenting the quest for a legitimate job through interviews with local providers of public goods and institutions related to employment.

2/Providers of public goods demonstrating in the streets of Berlin.

Shuichiro Yoshida
Tokyo, Japan

A volunteer group in Chikusei City in Ibaraki Prefecture, approximately 60 km north-east of Tokyo, Japan obtained a historic stone storage building, called 'Ishi-Kura', and maintains it as their base for discovering the regional historical and cultural heritages. Such buildings have existed in the region since early 20th century, although most were demolished and replaced by city development after the Second World War. Although the building, named Tokinokura, was in good condition and useful to the volunteer group, there were no lavatories for visitors or staff. In autumn 2008, the group organized a public design competition for the lavatories, which attracted 76 proposals. The winning design, by Shuichiro Yoshida, was built in February-May 2009. The small lavatory building includes two booths, one for men and one for women. Although the floor area is only 8.62 m², there is open space above the booths. It is intended that the lavatories are the start of a new history for Tokinokura and the region, preserving the region-specific landscape but also creating new landscape in the future. Lavatory visitors experience peace, enjoying the soft light from the upper window and the framed view of the old stone wall of Tokinokura.

Taketo Shimohigoshi
Tokyo, Japan

Taketo Shimohigoshi tries to bring more life to a high-density residential area in the heartland of Tokyo. Not on the ground level, where friendly streets with some degree of commercial facilities create an attractive atmosphere, but in the sky, which is cramped with endless continuation of detached appartment buildings. With little sign of people living inside, they seem to stand only as a manifold of separate inner spaces in mid-air Tokyo. As a code, all the apartments have balconies attached on the side, but they aren't actually being used, their mere purpose being to superficially show that the building has a residential function. Rather than becoming part of the living space, these balconies become barriers and close off the residents' lives from the outside. Without attractive exterior spaces, the atmosphere is dry and lifeless. Large beams are stretched between two white walls, covered with green moss. This green moss detached from the ground provides a new sense of perception to the urban fabric and the sky. Vegetation hanging in mid-air, where nature is not in its natural place, stirs imagination and sensuality. The vegetation becomes a buffer where ground is connected to the sky.

IC² Associated Architects
Brussels, Belgium

Everyone lives in a space that contains architecture and the public is not educated in this subject. It makes sense to start with children, to give them an understanding of the city, architecture and the arts in general. Bluub, a UFO in the city, designed by two architects, Ines Camacho and Isabelle Cornet, for children's educational workshops, can join architecture and arts activities in an independent way. It will catch the public's attention with its unusual shape and bright colour. This macro-object will be operational in June and can be moved all around Brussels, Belgium, and abroad. The word is a combination of 'Blub', the term for this specific form of architecture, and 'Hubble', the famous space telescope orbiting the planet. Bluub is a tool perfectly designed for children, made to their scale and containing all the elements necessary to organizing workshops and meetings. It can hold a dozen children and an activity leader, and transform itself according to the activity. Bluub can combine architecture and arts activities or work in an independent way. Its shape and colour might catch the eye of distant viewers and it was designed to attract a multicultural public. Bluub's impact on the landscape is remarkable, like a UFO that has landed, and when its mission is finished it is dismantled so that it can be installed again somewhere else.

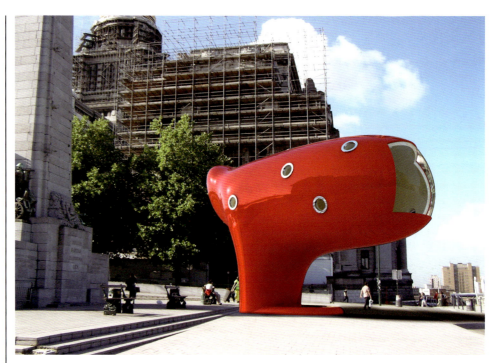

ProstoRož
Ljubljana, Slovenia

Since 2004, the ProstoRož association has aspired to exploring and understanding open city space. An ongoing project of public space cultivation, aiming to develop a method of reviving neglected urban spaces, it has intervened in city streets (parking interventions, customization of potential shop windows), created playgrounds and parks and renovated underpasses. ProstoRož explores, examines and opens new possibilities of public space use in accordance with the needs of residents. Sometimes, minimal means and small interventions are enough to present the city's inhabitants and visitors with pleasant spaces for hanging out, playing or working in the open air. Their interventions are not mere artistic installations in public areas; they also search thoroughly for new space use options. ProstoRož believes that in applying the appropriate approach to space planning, vandalism in public areas can be reduced.

1

2

3

1/3/Renovation of the Plečnik Underpass, Ljubljana.
2/ City Life project in the streets of Ljubljana.

José Luis Torres
Montmagny, Canada

With his 'Lieux de passages' installations, José Luis Torres proposes an inside-outside experiment that marks and exposes limits and borders, but that is also an installation in tune with the concept of displacement. Knowing that the search for a home and the concept of exile are same conditions of the existence, this installation attests that our constant displacements oblige us to rebuild our universe. Interaction with the spectator is at the core of this articulation, beginning with the random choreography of the walkers. The experiment of displacement thus makes it possible to consider mobility not according to the melancholic dimension of departure, but to the stimulating dimension of discovery, a gesture drawn from the transient which is integrated into the place in its temporary function.

Avi Laiser
Tel Aviv, Israel

For the 2008 Bat-Yam international Biennale of landscape, architect Avi Laiser created 'the REAL estate', a project that exploits 'edge conditions' in urban cities, which often create neglected public spaces that attract temporal activities of various kinds for a wide spectrum of people. Bat-Yam is one of Israel's most densely populated cities. Most residents live in modern housing projects that were built in the 1950s for new immigrants. The project is situated at the end of a wide modernist residential street that unexpectedly terminates with a massive concrete wall that functions as an acoustic highway barrier. This 'edge' creates a long strip of neglected 'junk' space used by residents for dumping trash, bonfires for Lag BaHomer (a Jewish holiday), drug activities, walking dogs and illicit behaviour. The REAL estate project creates an unusual public park that allows intimate/private human activities to exist in the public domain. It offers a new typology for public space that examines the boundaries between public and private domains in the urban landscape.

THE CITY AS CAN- VAS

Martin Bricelj
Ljubljana, Slovenia

RoboVox is a large (8-metre high) interactive public sound installation by media artist Martin Bricelj, using SMS for general public interaction. It will be installed in crowded metropolitan squares (Helsinki, Barcelona, Beijing, Paris, New York, Rotterdam, Berlin, etc.), preferably in those carrying some social or even political connotation. Its purpose is to serve as a tool for an individual, whose voice usually gets lost in the sounds of the masses. An individual can send a text message using his mobile phone to the RoboVox's number. Upon receiving the SMS RoboVox says out loud the statement, the protest, the declaration of love, or whatever the message may read, thus lending its voice to the anonymous individual.

Simon Siegman
Brussels, Belgium

For the festivities marking the launch of the Belgian presidency of the European Union, Simon Siegman proposed an urban scenography for the Flagey Square in Brussels. Called 'Mirror, Mirror', the proposition uses mirrors as a recurring material, covering the architecture to create a purified and ludic space that multiplies the spectator's points of view, offering him a new course and placing him within the heart of the device. The Art-Deco lines of the square's main building are highlighted by turning the building's windows into mirrors, reflecting the sunlight during the day and accentuating the building's dimensions at night with a great contre-jour, obtained by using blue and white lighting. On the square itself, a scene is framed by two mirrored walls, an alcove for artists and an enclosure for the public. The building and the square constitute the backbone of the project, with natural extensions in the adjacent Place Sainte Croix, where a large vertical mirror reflects Flagey, and the Ixelles Ponds, illuminated by submerged light sources that light up the surface of the water and the banks.

1

2

3

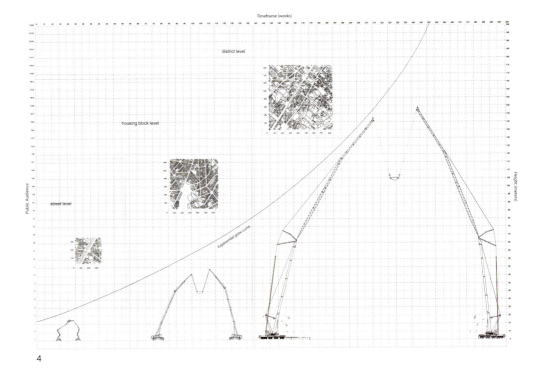

4

Gijs Van Vaerenbergh
1/ Spinoff 1, Micronomics festival 2008.
Picture Jeroen Verrecht.
2/3/ Projects for subsequent, bigger spiders.
4/ Diagram of the SpinOff project.

Gijs Van Vaerenbergh
Brussels, Belgium

The SpinOff project, by the Gijs Van Vaerenbergh duo (composed of Pieterjan Gijs and Arnout van Vaerenbergh) is a prime example of "city-hacking", by means of cranes, the very simple construction tools we use to build our cities. "They move through the urban skyline from one construction site to the next. They are symbols of the liveliness and self-renewing capacity of cities. What if these objects, normally used to construct cities, start using the city as their playground?" asks the duo. SpinOff is a generic concept for an urban installation that started with a small sketch of several assembled construction cranes that form a figure. What is fascinating is the ambiguity of the image: it shifts between cranes carrying an object on the one hand and a giant spider on the other. This spider could move through the city, from district to district. If quickly deconstructed and transported during the night, it could resurrect in a new neighbourhood the following morning, making it part of the urban skyline, animating urban life. To realize this, the project is being developed on different scales: the street, the urban block, the district and ultimately the city. Spinoff 1 is the realization on the smallest scale. Now Pieterjan and Arnout want to see the spider grow, as well as the resources, support and hype that go with it.

Cristina and Paula Neves
Porto, Portugal

Cristina (architect) and Paula (visual artist) were born in Venezuela, and now live and work in Porto, Portugal. For the city's D. João I square, they have imagined an installation — a rumination on the city, both visible and invisible, inhabited and uninhabited, and on humankind. It consists of printed vinyl and folded cardboard simulating a 3D human-scale figure placed on the square. The model silhouettes are placed perpendicular to the ground (cardboard figures) and horizontally as shadows (vinyl stickers). This ephemeral intervention is subject to weather and geographical conditions.

RE-IN-VENT-ING THE CITY

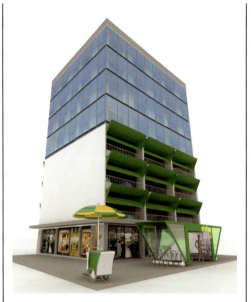

Maria Helena Coimbra Bueno (Baita design)
Rio de Janeiro, Brazil

With her Greener City project, Maria Helena Coimbra Bueno addresses the growing need to provide alternative energy to cities, reduce pollution and overdependence on non-renewable energy sources. It is composed of a self-sufficient building with funnel-shaped wind collectors on the parking levels, photovoltaic panels on the roof and green areas on rooftops and walls. There is a kiosk, and a reinvented shape for bus stops and bike stands.

Gia L. Daskalakis
Saint Louis, MO, USA

The Sutton Street Urban Fruit Garden project explores the interface between agriculture/ecology and new forms of activating public space. All cities have two footprints: the urban or constructed one and the ecological or natural one that extends beyond the urban, suburban and surrounding agricultural areas. As urban sprawl expands to consume agricultural land, that land in turn increasingly encroaches on sensitive wilderness ecosystems. Today, out of practical necessity and as a consequence of environmental imperatives, a new paradigm of local cultivation, integration and density is emerging. The idea of a new urban agriculture that is intertwined with the city's fabric is under careful consideration by a host of professionals including architects, urban designers, landscape architects, biologists, scientists, agronomists, etc.

Tspoon Environment Architecture
Rome, Italy

The limit between infrastructure and city is a space, an 'extra-space'. It's a territory inside the city with its own rules, directly connected to the neighbourhood's local scale, but at the same time related to a railway system that works on a metropolitan, regional and national scale. If we look at this territory as a continuous system of spaces that can redefine the relation between infrastructure and city, it can become a basic resource for city transformation and development. INFRACITTÁ is a hybrid space where it's possible to develop local resources and experiment with innovative instruments and practices in the search for a new relationship between city, nature, energy, mobility and communication on the metropolitan scale.

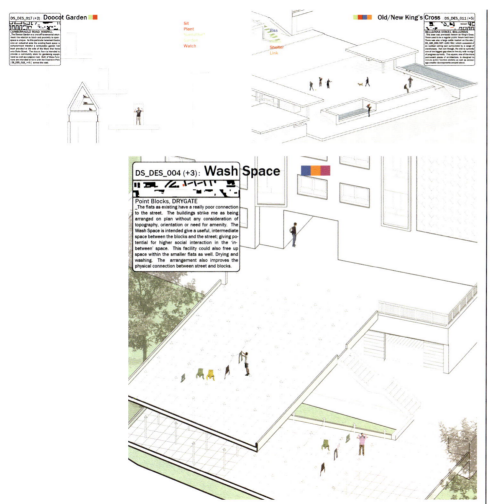

DS_DES_017 (+2) Doocot Garden

CUMBERNAULD ROAD, HIGHILL

Sit
Plant
Watch

Old/New King's Cross   DS_DES_011 (+5)

BELLGROVE STREET, BELLGROVE

Piss

Shelter
Link

DS_DES_004 (+3): Wash Space

Point Blocks, DRYGATE
_The flats as existing have a really poor connection
to the street. The buildings strike me as being
arranged on plan without any consideration of
topography, orientation or need for amenity. The
Wash Space is intended give a useful, intermediate
space between the blocks and the street; giving potential for higher social interaction in the 'in-
between' space. This facility could also free up
space within the smaller flats as well. Drying and
washing. The arrangement also improves the
physical connection between street and blocks.

Matt McKenna
Glasgow, United Kingdom

The Great Duke Street Digression is an
architectural project that explores existing
urban situations in order to develop a new type
of social infrastructure. It essentially looks
at how typological analysis and emotive (or
human) analysis can be combined to produce
a specific architectural insertion. A network
of small interventions was designed with the
analysis and themes driving the designs.
The designs were based on a temporary
architecture that would accommodate the
social functions for a number of years and –
depending on the outcome – could be made
a more permanent feature. The designs
were also planned in stages over a period of
five years in order to phase in the change,
potentially making changes to designs based
on observations. Also, on a practical level,
phasing the designs seemed more achievable.

Bibliography

AVV, *Urban Pioneers, temporary use and urban development in Berlin*, Senatsverwaltung fur Stadtentwicklung Berlin and Jovis Verlag Gmbh, Berlin, 2007.

Albrecht, D & E Johnson, *New Hotels for Global Nomads*, Merrell Publishers, London, 2002.

Appleyard, D, 'Why buildings are known. A predictive tool for architects and planners' in: G Broadbent, R Bunt & T Llorens (eds), *Meaning and behaviour in the built environment*, Wiley, Chichester, 1980.

ARENE, *Quartiers durables, guide d'expériences européennes*, ARENE, Ile de France, IMBE, April 2005, p. 128.

Arnstein, S, 'A Ladder of Citizen Participation' in: p. Le Gales & F Stout (eds.), *The City Reader*, Routledge, London, 2000, pp. 240-252.

Austin Turner, M, 'Urban Parks as Partners in Youth Development', in The Urban Institute and The Wallace Foundation brief *Beyond Recreation – A Broader View of Urban Parks*, 2004, pp. 1-7.

Avitabile, A, 'Le projet urbain : une culture du territoire et de l'action urbaine' in Y Chalas (ed.), *L'imaginaire aménageur en mutation*, l'Harmattan, Paris, 2004, pp. 25-38.

Bachelard, G, *La poetique de l'espace*, Quadrige, PUF, Paris, 1957.

Baek, JS, '*Designing collaborative services on the digital platform*', notes for a lesson at Politecnico di Milano in November 2009.

Banerjee, T & M Southworth, *City Sense and City Design: Writings and Projects of Kevin Lynch*, MIT Press, Cambridge, MA, 1991.

Barbara, A & A Perliss, *Invisible architecture. Experiencing Places through the Sense of Smell*, Skira, Milan, 2006.

Bauman, Z, *Liquid Modernity*, Polity Press, Malden, MA, Blackwell, Cambridge, 2000.

Bell, PA, JD Fisher, A Baum & TC Greene, *Environmental Psychology*, fifth edition, Thomson & Wadsworth, Belmont, CA, 2001.

Bitter, S & Weber, H, *Autogestion. Or Henri Lefebvre in New Belgrade*, Fillip Editions and Sternberg Press, Vancouver, New York, 2009.

Blondiaux, L, *La démocratie locale. Participation, représentation, espace public*, P.U.F., Paris, 1999.

Blondiaux, L, *Le nouvel esprit de la démocratie. Actualité de la démocratie participative*, Seuil, Paris, 2008.

Borasi, G, G Clement & P Rahm, *Environ(ne)ment,* Manières d'agir pour demain / Approaches for tomorrow, Skira, Milan, 2006.

Brat, Kind & Samenleving, '*Etude pour un redéploiement des aires ludiques et sportives en Région de Bruxelles-Capitale*', Project for the final report, IBGE, Brussels, 2009.

Bugarič, B, 'Procesi v mestnih jedrih : primer umeščanja univerzitetnega programa v historično mestno jedro Kopra', *Annales* 14, no. 2, 2004, pp. 409-428.

Careri, F, *Walkscapes, Camminare come pratica estetica*, Einaudi, Torino, 2006.

Cibic, A & L Tozzi, *Microrealities. A project about places and people*, Skira, Milan, 2006.

Coirier, L, *Label-Design in Belgium, Design in Belgium after 2000.* Stichting Kunstboek, Oostkamp, 2005.

Coirier, L, *Parckdesign, Embrassons les Arbres/Omhels de Bomen/Hug a Tree, Innovative urban furniture for parks*, Stichting Kunstboek, Oostkamp, 2007.

Collina, L & F Scullica, *Designing Designers. Designing hospitality: visions, scenarios, systems, services, spaces and products*, POLIdesign, Milan, 2005.

Cooper Marcus, C & C Francis (eds), *People Places: Design Guidelines for Urban Open Space*, second edition, John Wiley & Sons, Inc., Toronto, 1998.

Crasset, M, *Spaces 2000-2007*, Daab, Cologne, 2007.

Cullen, G, *Townscape*, Architectural Press, London, 1961.

Dall'Ara, G, *Programmare lo sviluppo turistico dei territori*, Editore Halley, Matelica, 2009.

De Bell, F, *Cascoland: Interventions in Public Space, Drill Hall, Johannesburg, South Africa*, Episode Publishers, Rotterdam, 2008.

Dear Architect, A vision of our new school, joint publication by Walker Technology College Newcastle, Engine Service Design, DOTT07, 2007.

Deleuze, G, 'Spazi nomadi, Figure e forme dell'etica contemporanea', *Millepiani*, no. 28, 2004.

Diers, J, *Neighbor Power, Building Community the Seattle Way*, University of Washington Press, Seattle and London, 2006.

Downs, RM & D Stea (eds), *Image and Environment. Cognitive Mapping and Spatial Behavior*, Aldine Pub. Co., Chicago, 1973.

Droog Design Foundation, Amsterdam, 2006.

Durance, P, D Kaplan, A Puissochet, & S Vincent, *Technologie et prospective territoriale*, Fyp Ed., Paris, 2008.

Edelkoort, L, Urban Oasis, in: *Bloom*, a horticultural view, Issue 14, Revenge, p. 146-151.

Elwood, S, 'Volunteered geographic information: key questions, concepts and methods to guide emerging research and practice', *GeoJournal*, no. 72, 2008, pp. 133-135.

Esterni, *Design Pubblico. Idee e progetti per lo spazio pubblico*, esterni, Milan, 2007.

Farinelli, F, 'Geografia. Un'introduzione ai modelli del mondo', Ed. Einaudi, Torino, 2003.

Filipovič Hrast, M & K Dekker, 'Old Habits Die Hard? Neighbourhood Participation in Post-WWII Neighbourhoods in Slovenia and the Netherlands', *Cities: The International Journal of Urban Policy and Planning*, vol. 26, no. 3, June 2009.

Frank, K A & Q Stevens (eds), *Loose space: Possibility and diversity in urban life*, Routledge, London, 2007.

Gastil, RW & Z Ryan (eds), OPEN. *New design for public space*, Van Alen Institute, New York, 2004.

Geddes, P, *Cities in Evolution, an introduction to the town planning movement and to the study of civics*, William & Norgate, London, 1915.

Gehl, J & L Gemzøe, *New City Spaces*, The Danish Architectural Press, Copenhagen, 2001.

Gehl, J, L Gemzoe, S Kirknaes & B Sternhagen Sondergaard, *New City Life*, The Danish Architectural Press, Copenhagen, 2006.

Genelot, S, *Quels aménagements pour les enfants et les jeunes. Territoires à vivre*, Questions d'éducation, France, 1998.

Gilles, C & L Jones, *Une écologie humaniste*, Aubanel, Paris, 2006.

Giono, J, *L'homme qui plantait des arbres*, Gallimard-Folio Cadet, Paris, 2006.

Goličnik, B & C Ward Thompson, 'Emerging relationships between design and use of urban park spaces', *Landscape and Urban Planning*, vol. 94, no. 19, 2010, pp. 38-53.

Goličnik, B & M Nikšič, 'Geographic information system behavioural and cognitive mapping in the city centre revitalisation process', *Journal of Urban Regeneration and Renewal*, vol. 3, no. 2, October-December 2009.

Goličnik, B, 'GIS behaviour mapping for provision of interactive empirical knowledge, vital monitoring and better place design' in S Porta, K Thwaites, O Romice & M Greaves (eds), *Urban Sustainability through Environmental Design: Approaches to time, people and place responsive urban spaces*, Routledge, Taylor & Francis, London 2007, pp. 136-140.

Goličnik, B, *People in place. A configuration of physical form and the dynamic patterns of spatial occupancy in urban open public space*, doctoral thesis, Edinburgh College of Art, Heriot Watt University, Edinburgh, 2005.

Goodchild, MF, 'Citizens as sensors: the world of volunteered geography', *GeoJournal*, no. 69, 2007, pp. 211-221.

Granovetter, M, 'The Strength of Weak Ties', *American Journal of Sociology*, vol. 78, no. 6, May 1973, pp. 1360-1380.

GreenKeys Project Team, *GreenKeys @ Your City – A Guide for Urban Green Quality*, IOER, Dresden, 2008.

Groupement des Coopératives d'habitation genevoises, *Cahier des charges pour un ecoquartier coopératif aux Communaux d'Ambilly*, 11 September 2007.

Gueben, G, *Choisir son mobilier urbain*, une sélection proposée par le ministère de l'Equipement et des Transports (MET), MET-UDB+, Namur, 1998-2001.

Halle, F, *Plaidoyer pour l'arbre*, Actes Sud, Paris, 2007.

Haydn, F & R Temel, *Temporary Urban Spaces. Concepts for the Use of City Spaces*, Birkhauser Verlag, Basel, 2006.

Hočevar, M, *Novi urbani trendi: prizorišča v mestih-omrežja med mesti*, Fakulteta za družbene vede, Ljubljana, 2000.

Huizinga, J, *Homo Ludens: A Study of the Play Element in Culture*, Beacon Press, Boston, 1955.

Hulot, N, *Pour un pacte écologique*, Calmann-Lévy, Paris, 2006.

Inghilleri, P, *La « buona vita ». Per l'uso creativo degli oggetti nella società dell'abbondanza*, Guerini e Associati, Milan, 2003.

IPoP, 'The role of civil society in urban planning', report, retrieved 15 April 2009.

Jacobs, J, *The Death and Life of Great American Cities*, Penguin Books, Harmondsworth, 1972.

Jégou F, J Liberman, S Girardi & A Bernagozzi, *Design for Social Innovation, Enabling replication of promising initiatives for sustainable living in Brussels and Paris*, Changing the Change design research conference, Torino, 2008.

Jégou, F & E Manzini (eds), *Collaborative Services, Social Innovation and Design for Sustainability*, Edizioni Poli. Design, Milan, 2008.

Jégou, F, V Thoresen & E Manzini, *LOLA Looking for Likely Alternatives. A didactic process for approaching sustainability by investigating social innovation*, Hedmark University College, Hamar, Norway, 2009.

Jones, JC, *Design Methods*, John Wiley and Sons, New York, 1992.

Jouen, M, *Des services publics à la conception des services au public*, Futuribles, 2009.

Kaplan, R & S Kaplan, *Experience of Nature: A Psychological Perspective*, Cambridge University Press, New York, 1989.

Kastner, J & B Walls, *Land Art et Art environnemental*, Phaidon, Paris, 2004.

Kattsoff, L, *The Design of Human Behavior*, Educational Publishers, St. Louis, 1947.

Kazazian, T, *Design et développement durable*, Il y aura l'âge des choses légères, Victoires-Editions, Paris, 2003.

Krauel, J, *New Urban Elements*, Links, Barcelona, 2007.

Križnik, B, *Kulturni okvir preobrazbe mest, lokalni odzivi na globalne izzive (primer Barcelone in Seula)*, doctoral thesis, University of Ljubljana, 2008.

Kvale, S, *InterViews. An introduction to Qualitative Research Interviewing*, SAGE Publications, Thousand Oaks, London, New Delhi, 1996.

Lacoste, Y, *La géographie ça sert d'abord à faire la guerre*, Maspero, Paris, 1976.

Landry, C, *The Creative City. A Toolkit for Urban Innovators*, Earthscan, London, 2000.

Le Maire, J & D Rouillard (dir.), *Grammaire de la participation. Théories et pratiques architecturales et urbanistiques. 1904-1968'*, doctoral thesis, art history, architecture division, Université Paris-Sorbonne, February 2009.

Leadbeater, C, *Personnalisation through participation. A new script for public services*, Demos, 2004.

Leadbeater, C, *We Think*, Profile Books, Ltd., London, 2008.

Lefebvre, H, *La production de l'espace*, Anthropos, Paris, 1974.

Lefebvre, H, *The Production of Space*, Blackwell, Oxford, 1991.

Leonard, D & J Rayport, 'Spark Innovation Through Empathic Design', *Harvard Business Review*, November-December 1997, pp. 102-113.

Lynch, K, *The Image of the City*, MIT Press, Cambridge, MA, 1960.

Lynch, K. (1981). *A Theory of good City Form*. Cambridge, Mass.: MIT Press.

Macauley, D, 'Walking the City' in *The Aesthetics of Human Environments*, A Berleant & A Carlson (eds), Broadview Press, Peterborough, 2007.

Manzini, E, 'Enabling solutions; Social innovation, creative communities and strategic design' and 'A cosmopolitan localism: Prospects for a sustainable local development and the possible role of design', 2005, http://sustainable-everyday.net, retrieved in March 2010.

Manzini, E., Small, Local, Open and Connected: Design Research Topics in the Age of Networks and Sustainability, in *Journal of Design Strategies*, Volume 4, No. 1, Spring 2010.

Marchal, M, *Quand l'Art épouse le Lieu*, MET, Namur, 1995.

Margolin, V, 'Design Studies in the Academy: Designing Our Future', CAA Annual Conference panel session closing remarks, 20 February 2003.

Merleau-Ponty, M, *Phenomenology of Perception*, Routledge, London, 2005.

Meroni, A & Sangiorgi, D, *Design for Services*, Gower Publishing, Ltd., Aldershot, 2010.

Meroni, A (ed.), *Creative Communities. People inventing sustainable ways of living*, Edizioni Polidesign, Milan, 2007.

Meroni, A, 'Strategic design: where are we now? Reflection around the foundations of a recent discipline', *Strategic Design Research Journal*, vol. 1, no. 1, July-December 2008, pp. 31-38 (Unisinos - Universidade do Vale do Rio dos Sinos, São Leopoldo, http://www.unisinos.br/sdrj).

Michelin, N, *Avis, propos sur l'architecture, la ville, l'environnement*, Archibooks + sautereau éditeur, Paris, 2006.

Mihelič, B, 'Geografski informacijski sistem kot orodje za analizo in vrednotenje stanja v prostoru ter določanje prioritetnih območij prenove / Geographical Information Systems as a tool for analyses and evaluation of physical conditions and determining priority areas for rehabilitation', *Urbani izziv*, vol. 16, no. 1, 2005, pp. 97-103.

Mihelič, B, I Bizjak, N Goršič, M Nikšič, I Stanič, B Cotič, B Tominc, D Zaviršek Hudnik, K Višnar, M Režek, *Prenova središča Ljubljane : metodologija za izdelavo projekta prenove karakterističnih območij in preizkus metodologije na pilotnem projektu prenove Miklošičevega parka / Rehabilitation of the city centre of Ljubljana: methodology for the elaboration of a project for the rehabilitation of characteristic areas and testing of the method in the case study area Miklošič'*, Urban Planning Institute of the Republic of Slovenia, Ljubljana, 2005.

Mihelič, B, R Sendi, B Černič Mali, I Bizjak, B Tominc & N Goršič, 'Prenova mesta: *Nabor inštrumentov za spodbujanje in izvajanje prenove / Renewal of cities: methodological tools for determination and evaluation of priority areas and types of renewal*, Urban Planning Institute of the Republic of Slovenia, Ljubljana, 2008.

Mitrasinović, M & K Salen, 'Playspace: A Case for Design Studies in Action', paper presented at the 4th International Conference on Design Studies and Design History, Guadalajara, Mexico, 1-5 November 2004.

Mitrasinović, M, *Total Landscape, Theme Parks, Public Space*, Ashgate, London, 2006.

Monmonier, M, *Spying with Maps: Surveillance Technologies and the Future of Privacy*, University Of Chicago Press, Chicago, 2002.

Morgan, L, *The Melrose malaise*. Los Angeles Reader, August 2, 10-14, 1996.

Mulgan, G, *Ready or not? Taking innovation in the public sector seriously*, Nesta, 2007.

Mulgan, G, *Social Innovation: what is it, why it matters, how it can be accelerated* The Young Foundation, London, 2006.

Mumford, L, *The City in History: Its Origins, Its Transformations, and Its Prospects*, Penguin Books, Middlesex, Harmondsworth, 1969.

Munari, B, *Disegnare un albero*, Edizioni Corraini, Mantova, 1978.

Murray, R, '*Danger and opportunity. Crisis and the new social economy*', Provocation 09, NESTA, UK, September 2009.

Murray, R, Mulgan, G & Caulier-Grice, J, '*How to Innovate: The tools for social innovation*', working paper. SIX, Social Innovation Exchange, UK, 2008.

Nikšič, M, *Povezovanje urbanih mikroambientov v prepoznavno celoto. Strukturiranost odprtega javnega prostora mesta v miselni sliki uporabnikov / Connecting urban microambients into a recognizable whole. Structure of open urban public space in mental image of users*, doctoral dissertation, University of Ljubljana, Ljubljana, 2008.

Nold, C (ed.), *Emotional cartography. Technologies of the self. A collection of essays*, http://www.emotionalcartography.net, retrieved November 2008.

O'Reilly, T, '*What Is Web 2.0, Design Patterns and Business Models for the Next Generation of Software*', http://oreilly.com/web2/archive/what-is-web-20.html, retrieved March 2010.

Pallasmaa, J., *The eyes of the skin. Architecture and the Senses*, Wiley, Chichester, 2005.

Passini, R, *Wayfinding in Architecture*, Van Nostrand Reinhold, New York, 1992.

Plateforme Flagey, 'Place à s'approprier. Quelle programmation pour la future Place Flagey?', 14 May 2007.

Preiser, W & E Ostoff (Eds), *The Universal Design Handbook*, McGraw-Hill, 2001.

Project for Public Spaces, *How to turn a place around: A handbook for Creating Successful Public Spaces*, PPS, New York, 2005.

Ramakers, R, & G Bakker, *The Human Touch*, Droog Design,

Randall, T, *Sustainable Urban Design*, An Environmental Approach. Taylor & Francis, London, 2003.

Rapoport, A, 'Cross-Cultural Aspects of Environmental Design' in A Rapoport, I Altman & JF Wohlwill (eds), *Human Behavior and Environment: Environment and Culture*, Plenum Press, New York, 1980.

Rapoport, A, *The Meaning of The Built Environment*, Sage Publications, Beverly Hills, 1982.

Rasmussen, SE, *Experiencing Architecture*, MIT Press, Cambridge, MA, 1964.

Raumlaborberlin, *Acting in Public*, Jonis Verlag GmbH, Berlin, 2008.

Register, R, *Ecocities*, Rebuilding Cities in Balance with Nature, New Society Publishers, Gabriola Island, 2006.

Relph, E, *Place and Placelessness*, Pion, London, 1976.

ReUrban Mobil: Reurbanization on the condition of demographic change (EU 5th Framework Programme, 2002-2005), http://www.re-urban.com, retrieved 7 February 2010.

Rienets, T, J Sigler & K Christiaanse, *Open City: Designing Coexistence*, Martien de Vletter, SUN, Amsterdam, 2009.

Salen, K & E Zimmerman, *Rules of Play: Game Design Fundamentals*, MIT Press, Cambridge, MA, 2004.

Scearce, D, K Fulton & the Global Business Network community, *What If? – The Art of Scenario Thinking for Nonprofits*, Global Business Network, Emeryville, 2004.

Schuiten, L & P Loze, *Archiborescence*, Mardaga, Sprimont, 2006.

Secrétariat régional au développement urbain (SRDU), 'Les projets socio-économiques réalisés dans le cadre des Contrats de Quartier', 17 June 2005 and 16 June 2006.

Seligman, MEP, & Csikszentmihalyi, M, 'Positive psychology: An introduction', *American Psychologist*, Vol. 55, pp. 5-14, 2000.

Slavid, R, Micro. *Very small buildings*, Laurence King Publishing, London, 2007.

SRDU, Secrétariat régional au développement urbain, 'Les projets socio-économiques réalisés dans le cadre des Contrats de Quartier', 17 June 2005 and 16 June 2006.

Stanič, I, 'Sinergija iz sodelovanja – zagotavljanje legitimnosti?', *Urbani Izziv*, vol. 16, no. 2, 2005.

Strelow, H, H Prigann & V David, *Ecological Aesthetics*, Art in Environmental Design: Theory and Practice. Birkhäuser, Reinach, 2004.

Sui, DJ, 'The wikification of GIS and its consequences: Or Angelina Jolie's new tattoo and the future of GIS', *ScienceDirect, Computers, Environment and Urban Systems*, no. 32, 2008, pp. 1-5.

Šuklje Erjavec, I et al., *Severni mestni park-Navje*, Ljubljana (design project and implementation documentation), MOL/URBI d.o.o., 1984-2009.

Šuklje Erjavec, I, 'Overlooked Potentials of Open Spaces: new types and categories of urban landscapes', *Urbani izziv*, vol. 2, no. 12, UIRS, Ljubljana, 2001.

Tapscott, D, & Williams, AD, 'Wikinomics 2.0: La collaborazione di massa che sta cambiando il mondo', Rizzoli-Etas, Milano, 2007.

Thakara, J, In the Bubble: Designing in a Complex World, MIT Press, Cambridge, 2005.

Thwaites, K & I Simkins, Experiential Landscape. An Approach to People, Place and Space, Routledge, London, New York, 2007.

Tiberghien, G A, Notes sur la nature, la cabane et quelques autres choses, Editions du Félin, Paris, 2005.

Toolkit to Address Wayfinding Problems' in B Martens & AG Keul (eds), Designing Social Innovation. Planning, Building, Evaluating, Hogrefe & Huber Publishers, Goettingen, 2005.

Tuan, Y, Space and Place. The Perspective of Experience, ninth edition, University of Minnesota, Minneapolis, 2002, first edition 1977.

Van Beckhoven, E, Decline and Regeneration: Policy responses to processes of change in post-WWII urban neighbourhoods, doctoral thesis, Utrecht University, 2006.

Van der Heijen, K, Scenarios: The Art of Strategic Conversation, John Wiley & Sons, West Sussex, 2005.

Van der Ryn, S & S Cowan, Ecological Design, Island Press, Washington D.C., 1995.

Von Bonsdorff, P, 'Urban Richness and the Art of Building' in Environment and the Arts: Perspectives on Environmental Aesthetics, A Berleant (ed.), Ashgate, Aldershot, 2002.

Von Vegesack, A & M Schwartz-Clauss, Living in Motion. Design and architecture for flexible dwelling, Vitra Design Museum, Weil am Rhein, 2002.

Ward Thompson, C, 'Urban open space in the 21st century', Landscape and Urban Planning, 60, 2002, pp. 59-72.

Ward Thompson, C, C Findlay & K Southwell, 'Lost in the Countryside. Developing a toolkit to address wayfinding problems'. In B Martens and G Keul Alexander (eds.) Designing Social Innovation: Planning, Building, Evaluating. Hogrefe & Huber Publishers, Göttingen, 2005.

Wheater, C P, Urban habitats, Routledge, London, 1999.

Whyte, WH, The Social Life of Small Urban Spaces, Conservation Foundation, Washington, D.C., 1980.

Woodworth, R, Dynamics of Behavior, Holt, New York, 1958.

Yota/Jes, Kinderparticipatie bij de vormgeving van de publieke ruimte, Belgium, 2009.

On-line sources:

www.abc-web.be
www.albergodiffuso.com
www.childfriendlycities.eu
www.childfriendlycities.org
www.childinthecity.com
www.designcamping.it
www.dott07.com/go/designcampprojects
www.emotionalcartography.net
www.estaesunaplaza.blogspot.com
www.greenkeys-project.net
www.jes.be
www.karakol.be
www.k-s.be
www.m-hotel.org
www.microcompacthome.com
www.microrealities.org
www.openlayers.org.
www.openstreetmap.org
www.polok.si
www.shirky.com
www.sust.org/?view=45&parent=3
www.sustainable-everyday.net
www.turtlewings.be
www.wiels.org

About the authors

Boštjan Bugarič is a researcher at the Science and Research Centre of Koper at the University of Primorska. He established an independent group of artists, KUD C3, that works with public space projects. His field of research is public space, development of the contemporary city, public involvement and study of social changes in the city.

Aidan Cerar is a sociologist trained at the University of Ljubljana and Universität Lüneburg. He has worked with the Urban Planning Institute of the Republic of Slovenia and the British Council. Currently, he is pursuing his PhD and is a researcher at the Institute for Spatial Policies, IPoP. He is involved in international projects dealing with urban regeneration and civic participation in spatial planning, and with Prima Architects as an adviser in architecture competitions.

Lise Coirier has developed Pro Materia Association since 1999 in Belgium and internationally. She is actively promoting contemporary design with a large focus on the city environments and its socio-cultural impact (EDF-Designing public spaces and mobility, Human Cities Concept and Festival, Parckdesign competition, Commerce Design award). With both Masters in Management and Art History, she is also a driving force of many workshops and symposiums. She writes books and curates exhibitions and is a publisher and an editor in chief of TL Magazine which shapes tomorrow's trends and living.

Luisa Collina, an architect with a PhD, is a professor of design at Politecnico di Milano. Her main interests are strategic design and design driven system innovation, with a focus on retail and hospitality. Since 2000 she has led international design projects and is member of the PhD design board at Politecnico di Milano. Since 2005, she has chaired an English-language product-service-system design master's programme designed for international students.

Elisabetta Fanti studied humanities and has worked at *esterni* since 2004 on the creative development of several projects. She is now head of the Communication Department and artistic director of the Milano Film Festival. For this reason she watches approximately 1,000 films a year.

Giordana Ferri holds a degree in architecture from Politecnico di Milano. She is the Head of Research and Planning for the Social Housing Foundation, which develops the master plans for new residential dwellings. She has been a visiting Service Design Professor for the Facoltà del Design, Politecnico di Milano, since 2006. In recent years, she has been involved in service design for residential dwellings, focusing on building co-housing projects and experimental programmes involving resident participation. She is a member of the Service Design Commission for the Compasso D'Oro Prize.

Barbara Goličnik Marušić holds a PhD in landscape architecture from the Edinburgh College of Art, Heriot Watt University, Edinburgh, UK. She is a landscape architect and researcher at the Urban Planning Institute of the Republic of Slovenia and an assistant professor at the School of Architecture at the University of Maribor, Slovenia. She is mainly involved in multidisciplinary national and international studies and projects concerned with design and research addressing environment-behaviour issues in the context of urban planning and open space design. She is a member of the international networks UStED and IAPS.

Nina Goršič is an architect at the Urban Planning Institute of the Republic of Slovenia. She is involved in national and international research and applied projects related to large housing estates, re-urbanization of inner city residential areas, urban cultural heritage and accessibility of urban environments for disabled people. She is also skilled in exhibition design and graphic and Internet design.

Sabine Guisse is an architect who graduated from La Cambre in 2005. Since January 2006, she has been working as a researcher at the *Centre de Recherches Architecturales de la Cambre* (CRAC), as part of the Prospective Research for Brussels programme supported by the Brussels region. Her research project focuses on the use of public space and its recognition as a resource for design. It is one of the main theoretical contributions to the European project Human Cities. By maintaining the question of usage as a backdrop, she set up the colloquium 'Places to be', part of the Human Cities Festival.

Rafaella Houlstan-Hasaerts graduated from the La Cambre Institute of Architecture (Brussels) in 2007. Since then, she has been collaborating with the not-for-profit organizations Recyclart, City Mine(d), and Constant and the graphic designers of Speculoos on the project 'Towards a subjective collective cartography'. At La Cambre, she is currently researching objects that define the public space in the Brussels Region and the ways actors and receptors qualify or disqualify those objects.

François Jégou, director of the Brussels design research company Strategic Design Scenarios, has experience in strategic design, participative scenario-building and new product-services system definition. He is active in various projects from investigating *Creative Communities for Sustainable Living* in China, India, Brazil and Africa with UNEP, to a European research project building a deliberative platform on food and nanotechnology. He is scientific director of the public innovation laboratory *27e Région* in France and teaches strategic design at the Politecnico, Milan, and La Cambre, Brussels.

Kathy Madden is an environmental designer who has been at PPS since its inception in 1975. During this time, Kathy has directed over 300 researches and urban design projects along with training programs throughout the U.S and abroad. She also currently directs PPS's Placemaking Training and Public Space Research and Publications programs. Prior to working at PPS, Kathy worked at the Institute for Architecture and Urban Studies and at the New York City Parks Department where she conducted an evaluation of park equipment and street furniture.

Judith le Maire holds a PhD in Architecture from Paris 1 La Sorbonne (Participative Grammar. Theories and practices in architecture and urbanism.

1904-1968, 2009). She is coordinator for the Centre de Recherches Architecturales de La Cambre in Brussels. She also teaches architecture.

Nicolas Malevé has been a data activist since 1998 and has been a member of the association Constant, organizing activities regarding alternatives to copyrights, such as Copy.cult & The Original Si(g)n, held in 2000. He develops multimedia projects and web applications for cultural organizations. His research work is currently focused on cartography, information structures, metadata and the means to visually represent them. He lives and works in Barcelona and Brussels.

Ezio Manzini is a Professor of Design at the Politecnico di Milano, Honorary Doctor at The New School of New York (2006) and at the Goldsmiths College of London (2008) and honorary professor at the Glasgow School of Art (2009). His main interests are design for social innovation and sustainability and he is the coordinator of DESIS, an international network focused on this topic (http://www.desis-network.org). Recent publications: Collaborative services (Polidesign, Milano, 2008) and Manzini, E, 'Small, Local, Open and Connected' in *Journal of Design Strategies*, vol. 4, no. 1, spring 2010.

Anna Meroni works as a researcher in the Department INDACO (Industrial Design) of Politecnico di Milano, where she is also assistant professor of service and strategic design. Co-director of the international Master Degree Programme in Strategic Design, she is a visiting professor and scholar in other schools and universities. Her research topics are service design and strategic innovation towards sustainability, with an emphasis on social innovation. She has considerable research experience in projects for sustainable urban and regional development conducted with a design approach.

Breda Mihelič holds a PhD in the History of Art, is acting director of the Urban Planning Institute of Slovenia and an assistant professor at the University of Primorska. Her research has involved theoretical and empirical studies of the history of architecture and town planning, urban morphology and architectural typology, and methodologies of urban rehabilitation and conservation. She is the author of several books and articles on urban and architectural history, collaborates on different international research projects and is a board member of the international association Reseau Art Nouveau Network.

Miodrag Mitrasinović is an architect, urbanist, author and Dean of The School of Design Strategies, Parsons The New School for Design. He is the author of Total Landscape, Theme Parks, Public Space (Ashgate 2006), and co-editor of Travel, Space, Architecture (Ashgate 2009). Both books are recipients of the Graham Foundation Grant in 2004 and 2005. He is a member of the advisory board of Design and Culture (Berg). His work continues to be focused on new ways of understanding, engaging with, and acting in relation to emerging urban processes, practices, phenomena, forms and conditions.

Matej Nikšič is an architect and holds an MA in urban design from Oxford Brookes University and a PhD in architecture from the University of Ljubljana. He works as a researcher at the Urban Planning Institute of the Republic of Slovenia. He is involved in national and international basic and applied research projects, and is expert in the fields of detailed urban design and place identity by design. His current research focuses on open urban public spaces in general and user mental images of them in particular.

Marko Peterlin of the Institute for Spatial Policies-IPoP is an architect trained at the University of Ljubljana. He obtained his master's degree in architecture and urban culture from the Technical University of Catalonia in Barcelona. He focuses on spatial and urban development policies and strategic planning, and has worked on INTERREG, ESPON and national applied research projects. His practical experience with the institutional and political aspects of Member States stems from the Ministry of the Environment and Spatial Planning of Slovenia, where he collaborated in many working groups.

Giampiero Pitisci studied industrial design, philosophy and socio-cultural anthropology, with specific interests in design methodology, aesthetics and semiotics, ethnographic tools and economic anthropology. From a classical product design-based education, he progressively turned to product-service design and projects investigating design impact in social innovation strategies. He collaborates regularly with Strategic Design Scenarios, Brussels.

Scott G. Pobiner is an Assistant Professor of Information, Design, and Management and former BBA Director at Parsons The New School for Design. Dr. Pobiner holds a doctorate from the Harvard University Graduate School of Design (2010) where he studied the relationship between display technology, interaction, and pedagogy in design education. Dr. Pobiner also holds a Master of Design Studies degree from Harvard University (2003) and a Bachelor of Architecture from Cornell University's School of Architecture, Art and Planning (2001).

Serena Pollastri graduated from Politecnico di Milano in 2009, where she studied service design and wrote a thesis on collaborative maps for service design. With Alta Scuola Politecnica, she worked on a project for the sustainable development of an informal settlement in Ecuador. After collaborating with Poli.Design as a strategic designer, and with Politecnico di Milano as assistant to the didactic activity, she focused on social innovation and environmental sustainability. She is now a senior researcher for Tektao Studio, Shanghai.

Anna Spreafico has worked for *esterni* since 2003. She focuses on the development of long-term projects in public spaces, dealing with public institutions. Since 2007, she has coordinates the *Design Pubblico* project and the Public Design Festival.

Eduardo Staszowski is an Assistant Professor and Coordinator of Academic Projects and Partnerships at the School of Design Strategies at Parsons The New School For Design. Co-founder of the DESIS Lab at The New School his research focuses on the use of design to generate social change and the improvement of the local environment.

Ina Šuklje Erjavec holds an M.Sc in Landscape Architecture from the University of Ljubljana. She is licensed landscape architect and spatial planner, a senior researcher at the Urban Planning Institute of the Republic of Slovenia and a leader of several projects at national and international level. She has extensive research experience in the theoretical and empirical studies of urban landscape planning and design, developing urban landscape planning, and design guidance and methodologies.

Biba Tominc is a geographer working at the Urban Planning Institute of the Republic of Slovenia. She participates in multidisciplinary projects and research in the field of urban planning, urban renewal and cultural heritage. Her main focus areas are GIS software programmes and information design. She specializes in data visualization, database creation, analysis and management and explores how to demonstrate spatial data in clear, effective and friendly way for different users and different media.

Paola Trapani, an architect with a PhD in industrial design, is interested in the use of ICT technologies to support community development and social innovation. She is specialized in scenario techniques, service notation tools and participative design approaches to ensure final user engagement in effective product/service system development. She collaborates as a researcher and adjunct professor with Politecnico di Milano, Università degli Studi di Milano and Università Cattolica del Sacro Cuore.

Chantal Vanoeteren studied management and town planning. After several years in sales and marketing, she specialized in sustainable development and town planning through professional experiences with local, regional and federal authorities, within research teams and for a consultancy office. In collaboration with Pro Materia she launched the Human Cities concept. She is currently working at the ISACF-La Cambre in Brussels where she coordinates the Human Cities project and works on [pyblik], a professional training centred on urban public spaces.

Stéphane Vincent has been working in innovation in the French public sector since 1995. After 15 years in local governments and consultancy, he initiated the research programme *27e Région*, which promotes design and social innovation in administrations and governments. A 2005 German Marshall Fund Fellow, he specializes in digital media, public policy and management.

Colophon

Editors
Barbara Goličnik Marušić, Matej Nikšič, Urban Planning Institute of the Republic of Slovenia; Lise Coirier, Pro Materia

Editorial Board
Barbara Goličnik Marušić, Matej Nikšič, Urban Planning Institute of the Republic of Slovenia; Lise Coirier assisted by Zoé Vantournhoudt, Pro Materia; Gian Giuseppe Simeone, Culture Lab

Contributing authors (Parts I, II, III)
Boštjan Bugarič, Aidan Cerar, Lise Coirier, Luisa Collina, Elisabetta Fanti, Giordana Ferri, Barbara Goličnik Marušić, Nina Goršič, Sabine Guisse, Rafaella Houlstan-Hasaerts, François Jégou, Kathy Madden, Judith le Maire, Ezio Manzini, Anna Meroni, Nicolas Malevé, Breda Mihelič, Miodrag Mitrasinović, Matej Nikšič, Marko Peterlin, Giampiero Pitisci, Scott G. Pobiner, Serena Pollastri, Ana Spreafico, Eduardo Staszowski, Biba Tominc, Paola Trapani, Chantal Vanoeteren, Ina Šuklje Erjavec, Stéphane Vincent.

We also thank the authors of the selected projects within the call for entries "Places to be" (Part IV): Maria Helena Coimbra Bueno - Baita design, Fédérica Zama, Christopher Patten, Gia L. Daskalakis, Bendan Cormier, Association Inscrire - Françoise Scheine, Markus Miessen, Petra Kempf, Matt McKenna, Lucile Soufflet, Taketo Shimohigoshi, Beate Lendt, Stephanie Carleklev, José Luis Torres, Christina & Paula Neves, Cristina de Almeira, Irena Paskali, Martin Bricelj, Gijs Van Vaerenbergh, IC² Associated Architects – Isabelle Cornet & Ines Camacho, ProstoRož, City Mine(d), Swati & Shruti Janu, Hana Miletic, Avi Laiser, Orna Marton, Shuichiro Yoshida, Nicolo Piana, Tspoon environment architecture, Simon Siegmann.

Copyediting
Lee Gillette

Final editing
Heide-Mieke Scherpereel, Stichting Kunstboek

Graphic design
Biba Tominc, Damjan Jermančič, Nina Goršič, Urban Planning Institute of the Republic of Slovenia; Guillaume Bokiau

Cover
Guillaume Bokiau. Picture Chantal Vanoeteren

This publication has been released in the framework of the European project Human Cities: Celebrating public space (2008-2010). It has been launched at the Human Cities Festival, Brussels (BE), 6-16 May 2010.

The contributions to this book have been peer reviewed.

We thank all the contributors for the pictures provided free of copyright.

ISBN 978-90-5856-345-3
D/2010/6407/9
NUR: 656

Printed by Pure Print (BE)
www.pureprint.be

This book is co-published by Stichting Kunstboek, www.stichtingkunstboek.com Urban Planning Institute of the Republic of Slovenia, www.uirs.si Pro Materia, www.promateria.be

© Stichting Kunstboek, April 2010.

This project has been funded with support from the European Commission - Programme Culture 2007-2013. This publication reflects the views only of the authors, and the Commission cannot be held responsible for any use which may be made of the information contained therein.

HUMAN CITIES / celebrating public space
www.humancities.eu